MW00980899

HOLDING THE HEAD

HOLDING THE HEAD

Michael Ashton

THE CHRISTADELPHIAN
404 SHAFTMOOR LANE
HALL GREEN
BIRMINGHAM B28 8SZ

2009

First Edition: 2009

© 2009 The Christadelphian Magazine & Publishing Association Limited

ISBN 978-085189175-X

Printed and bound by

THE CROMWELL PRESS GROUP
TROWBRIDGE
WILTSHIRE
ENGLAND
BA14 0XB

CONTENTS

FOREWORD

DISCIPLESHIP is all about following. There could be no disciples unless there was a Master, and no followers unless there was a Leader. The Lord is Master and Leader of each individual disciple, but also of many disciples, who together form his body: a worldwide community of believers devoted to his service.

Each disciple serves the Lord while living among those who generally have no regard for him, and whose motivations are often contrary to the principles he taught. True believers focus always on his example, so that issues of life are seen if at all possible as he would see them, so that God's name is honoured in every aspect of life. His motivation was always to do his Father's will, and he set the example so that others might "follow his steps".

The relationship between disciples and the Lord is therefore described in scripture as one between the body of believers and its head, who is Christ. Disciples are encouraged at all times to think of him if they are to grow to be more like him. This idea of growth is of spiritual maturity, adopting the Lord's mind: his thinking and his ways.

The material in this book considers the importance of this scriptural theme as it is expanded, mainly in the writings of the apostles. It was originally published as a monthly series in *The Christadelphian*, (August 2005 – December 2006). These articles have been extended and revised and are presented now in the hope that they will assist every disciple to follow the Lord Jesus more closely, until he comes in power and glory to establish his Father's kingdom.

MICHAEL ASHTON

1

"FOLLOW ME"

THEY are only two words, but they are among the hardest and the most rewarding in all the scriptures. To those who would be his disciples, the Lord Jesus said, "Follow me". He then proceeded to set an example that none of his disciples has ever come close to approaching. Yet the call still sounds forth, and followers of Jesus "press toward the mark for the prize of the high calling of God in Christ Jesus". As runners in the race for life eternal they must strain every sinew, keep their eyes fixed on the joy set before them, and be totally reassured of victory by "looking to Jesus the pioneer and perfecter of faith".

Theory and practice do not always coincide, however, and every disciple experiences times when the concentration slips, times when the focus is not clearly on the Lord and the kingdom to come. The world tries to press all its sons into its mould, and worldly pressures quickly claim attention and divert the energies from the pursuit of godliness. Without constant vigilance the grip on heavenly things loosens, and instead of holding fast to the Head, the disciple finds himself in the grip of other claims upon his time, his energy and his passions.

Taking stock

The objective of this short work is to sound a call for individual reassessment and communal realignment. Machinery needs periodic re-calibration, disciples need to take stock regularly of where they stand in relation to the Lord and his Father's purpose, and the brotherhood in his name should always be looking to "grow up into him in all things, which is the head, even Christ".

Every age has its difficulties; they may differ in nature, but the effects are the same. The hold on faith is loosened, and the vision of the future is dimmed. It happened in the lives of the first man and the first woman, even though they lived in a much more perfect environment than the one that presently exists. Throughout subsequent human history, the effects of sin have eaten away at the commitment of the best of men, save the One who stands supreme.

Temptation and sin

Sin is the major barrier preventing disciples from closely following their Lord, for it so easily besets humankind. No individual is free from the constant pressure of temptation to sin; it arises in the form of lusts that war in our members, and many, many battles in that war are lost. Thankfully, the Captain of our salvation opened up a way of escape, through overcoming sin on its own battlefield – our common humanity. As a consequence of his great victory, disciples receive the forgiveness of their sins at baptism "for his sake", and each time they repent and seek forgiveness: for "the blood of Jesus Christ cleanses from all sin".

As if the daily struggle against individual temptations were not enough, each believer lives in a desperately sinful environment. For many disciples, the pressures of the current age come from prevailing apathy, contempt and ridicule. Perhaps never before in the history of the world has there been so little acknowledgement of the existence of God, or so much blasphemy of His name in word and deed. Daily exposure to this constant erosion of godly values can quickly blunt the senses, and dull the edge of consciences whet sharp by the message of the scriptures, for "friendship with the world is enmity with God" (James 4:4). Each disciple should take stock regularly, and ask if he is following his Lord as closely today as he chose to follow him on entering the waters of baptism.

The Apostle Peter recognised the problem: "For to this you were called", he said, "because Christ also suffered for us, leaving us an example, that you should follow his steps" (1 Peter 2:21). He understood that the call demands a following; it is imperative, leaving no doubt what is required of those who hear. Nor are disciples left to choose how best to follow; Jesus provided an example. No resistance, no scorn, no threat or suffering for conscience sake should divert the disciple from his intended course. The example stands supreme. Jesus, "when he was reviled, did not revile in return; when he suffered, he did not threaten".

Following the Lord closely has serious implications. Disciples will not be spared the testing of suffering and disappointment, but God has promised with every temptation "the way of escape, that you may be able to bear it". So when a disciple suffers for well doing, it is acceptable to God because that was Jesus' way.

The dangers of ecumenism

As well as the pressures of worldliness, there are other things that drag disciples away from the Lord's footsteps. As the world grows ever more godless, differences between those who claim to follow Christ can seem less significant. It can be tempting to find common cause with anyone who chooses to stand aside from rampant materialism or outright wickedness and look for the spiritual values of life. The argument put forward by their adversaries in the days of the returning exiles, that "we seek your God, as you do", is still current today. But the ecumenical call to forget – and not to resolve – long held differences, draws disciples away from, and not closer to their Lord and to his truth. True unity is found only through him: by learning more about him, being more aware of his grace and more constant in devotion to his example.

In choosing to become one of his disciples, believers are constituent members of his body. Their acceptance of the call is an individual matter, but in accepting it they become living stones that are being built into a dwelling place of God through the Spirit. They are individually members one of another. The Apostle Paul told believers in Corinth who, for various reasons were not united around the person of their Saviour, "You are not your own ... [there are] many members, yet one body". This teaching runs directly counter to the spirit of this modern age, with its emphasis on individuals' rights and its encouragement to seek self-fulfilment above all else. Disciples follow the Lord in company with, and not by standing aside from, their fellow disciples.

The family of Christ is therefore a community of people, and not a haphazard collection of individuals. Through his association with fellow believers each believer learns the lesson about bearing one another's burdens, of being "like-minded toward one another, according to Christ Jesus, that you may with one mind and one mouth glorify the God and Father of our Lord Jesus Christ" (Romans 15:5,6).

God is not glorified, therefore, by disciples who try to redefine Christ's family by drawing in some who are not truly his; or by those who choose to respond to difficulties by peremptorily cutting off and never allowing the healing balm of God's word to bring peace. Believers are called to follow in the footsteps of the Prince of Peace by being peacemakers themselves. The call to discipleship is therefore a challenge to each believer to practise the Lord's sacrificial attitude: "Because he laid down his life for us ... we also ought to lay down our lives for the brethren" (1 John 3:16).

The author of salvation

Jesus did not turn from us in our hour of need, but sought to draw us close to him. He did not alter, or treat as irrelevant his Father's commands; nor did he erect new barriers to prevent our access to God, but positively worked to remove the ones that existed. When the Apostle Paul had to define the essence of the

Gospel message in difficult conditions in Corinth, he did not hesitate to say that, "Christ died for our sins according to the scriptures". The whole of the Father's eternal purpose turns on this great truth, for only through the Lord's selfless sacrifice can God's name be glorified. The declaration is right at the heart of godly faith, explaining man's need and God's response, and how the Lord Jesus was perfectly fitted to be the author of salvation.

The nearer each believer comes to these great truths, the more impact they have on his thoughts, and his way of life. He is called upon to reflect the spiritual character of his Saviour, and this demands doing everything possible to correct, restore and assist – fruitful consequences of spiritual perception. Away from Christ is the breeding ground for the works of the flesh, like anger, strife, division, and discord. It is not possible to produce both fruit and works; it must be God or mammon, flesh or spirit, law or grace. By being in Christ a disciple is raised high above the levels of human thinking, and is led to the throne room of heaven itself. The greatest honour is to live by the heartbeat of God's word, just as the Lord Jesus' meat and drink was to do the will of his Father who sent him.

Christlike thinking

The example of the Lord Jesus Christ has therefore to become the centre and pivot of each disciple's life. Straying from that centre will put his life out of balance, even though the effects may not be immediately apparent; but like an unbalanced machine, centrifugal forces will soon reveal potential disaster. The importance of this centre to life can be seen in the millions upon earth who live aimlessly, like vessels adrift on an ocean of despair. The life of Jesus and the hope centred on him provide a sure and steadfast anchor in all the storms of life. Confidence in that centre breeds conviction, and conviction confession: "there is no other name under heaven given among men by which we must be saved" (Acts 4:12).

Times arise in every believer's life when he feels under pressure. It may be a personal weakness, concern about a loved one, tension within family or ecclesia, a challenge to faith from outside or inside the brotherhood, disillusionment because of the behaviour of one previously held in high regard, unreasonable demands of worldly employers, financial straitness, disappointment at the apparent delay in Christ's return, or any of a vast number of different difficulties that can arise in daily life. The only answer in all such situations is to apply Christlike thinking; to get close to the Saviour in every possible way. To move away from him is to lose focus and direction. Clarity and guidance come from looking through his eyes, and realising how every human problem finds its solution only through God's word becoming flesh.

Each difficulty and problem, whatever its nature, is another call to follow Jesus, and to keep following. Disciples are called to overcome, yet quickly learn that it is an impossible task unaided. Any and every victory is his: sins are forgiven for his sake; temptations are overcome by the power of God's word and the Lord's example; problems are put into perspective through relating them to his sacrifice; strife is ended by the quiet voice of the Prince of Peace.

2

ONE HEAD

DISCIPLES of Christ constitute the Lord's earthly body and, in the figurative language of the Apostle Paul, are all "members individually" of his body. This relationship is critical. Naturally speaking, the head controls every thought, movement and action of the body, and the same is intended to apply to a disciple's spiritual life; he should be governed by the Lord who is his head. The body can survive and operate if limbs or even certain organs are missing, but the head is crucial. It is the control tower, directing everything the body does.

The analogy of the Christ-body reveals a number of different aspects that can be beneficially considered. There can be no better place to start than to concentrate on the fact that the Lord is its head. For though "the body has many members", there is only one head, and that is Christ.

This was Jesus' destiny before ever he was born. He was "made to have dominion". God "put all things under his feet". Though he was the Son and heir, it remained a position that he had to earn. While it is distasteful to consider defeat, it must be acknowledged that the possibility of failure existed throughout his mortal life. Jesus could have followed his own desires, ignored his Father's will, grasped prematurely for equality, or chosen to enjoy the pleasures of sin for a season. Knowing about his planned destiny did not smooth the path to victory, as his agony in the garden showed only too clearly. He wrestled day and night with the same temptations that press upon all his disciples, overcoming them only by heeding his Father's word and by delighting in His law.

"He humbled himself"

Scripture therefore confirms that only the humble and submissive are truly exalted: "Whoever exalts himself will be humbled, and he who humbles himself will be exalted" (Matthew 23:12). And the Lord never expects anything of his disciples that he did not first accomplish himself. Paul therefore explains that, "being found in appearance as a man, he humbled himself and became obedient to the point of death, even the death of the cross. Therefore God also has highly exalted him and given him the name which is above every name" (Philippians 2:8,9).

Pride and self-seeking attitudes are therefore totally inconsistent with membership of the Lord's body. His call is directed instead to the poor in spirit, those that mourn, the meek, they that hunger and thirst after righteousness, the merciful, the pure in heart, the peacemakers, and those that are persecuted for righteousness' sake. No wonder "not many wise according to the flesh, not many mighty, not many noble, are called". No flesh should glory in the presence of God who sent His Son to be Lord of lords and King of kings.

There is therefore a certain attitude of mind required of disciples, which Paul describes as "the mind of Christ". One way that disciples reveal this mind is if they truly consider that the Lord is the head of the body. He is peerless. He is head because he is "the beginning, the firstborn from the dead, that in all things he may have the preeminence" (Colossians 1:18). The reference here to Jesus as "the beginning" is particularly helpful, for the Apostle uses the word in the sense of referring to one who holds the highest and therefore the first place. Two more references help to make this point. The letter to the Laodiceans was written by "the Amen, the faithful and true witness, *the beginning* of the creation of God" (Revelation 3:14). This explains that God's purpose will be fulfilled through His "new" creation, which is headed by the Lord Jesus

Christ; and this has been made sure because Jesus is "the firstborn from the dead". Disciples will receive the kingdom and eternal life only through him and through his selfless and humble obedience. He was the firstfruits of a harvest that has yet to be gathered in. His work will not be completed until what he started is brought to its final conclusion. Jesus is therefore described as "the Alpha and Omega, the Beginning and the End" (22:13).

Two extremes

Yet it is possible, even for those who claim to be the Lord's disciples, for his headship to be denied in practice. Describing two extremes that occur from time to time will help to make this point. One of these extremes, while acknowledging the importance of the Lord's work for mankind, elevates something else to a higher position than the one the Lord Jesus currently occupies, seated at the right hand of God. This was apparent in the times of the apostles, and still exists today despite all the New Testament evidence of its dangers. What is elevated to the point where it displaces the Lord himself is "law". First century disciples with a Jewish background did not find it easy to break free from their system of law to enter into "the liberty by which Christ has made us free" (Galatians 5:1). It can be equally hard today, and the failure fully to accept the headship of Christ hides behind the cloak of dogma, insistence on specific wording, making the rule more important than the principle on which it is based, effectively ignoring the importance of mercy, longsuffering and gentleness.

System or Saviour

The Lord's condemnation of those in his day who tithed all manner of herbs, and passed over judgement and the love of God, should show that the same problem can exist today. Some may ask how this extreme is recognised. It exists when the truth is claimed to be a formula of words rather than a life governed by the mind of Christ; when greater attention is paid to cutting off than to searching out the lost and weary; to exposing errors in the body than to preaching to those who are still in darkness; when more emphasis is placed on the outward appearance than on the heart; when, to prevent being contaminated, those who need urgent help are ignored; when the evils in the world are tackled by a policy of isolation and conservatism, as if exclusiveness is equivalent to holiness. It exists in the minutiae of constitutions, committees, minutes and statements, when these prevent brotherly dialogue and joyful discussion of the living word; when isolation is preferred to sweet fellowship; when the Lord, who is the head, is rarely seen as a living Saviour, but only through types, shadows and symbols. The system eventually obscures and silences the Saviour.

There is another extreme that also denies the headship of the Lord, and it too existed in the first century ecclesia. As the Preacher said, there is no new thing under the sun. Those who form this extreme do not replace the Lord with another head. The problem here is that they make the Lord subject to the body, rather than the body subject to the head. One character is mentioned in the New Testament ecclesia because he loved to have the preeminence among them. Diotrephes would certainly not claim to have demoted the Lord; doubtless he would call the Lord's teaching in support of his own viewpoint. But the effect of his failure truly to honour the Son meant that membership of the body of Christ was not sufficient for him. He was prepared to exclude even the Lord's apostles from his assembly! Treating Christ as head demands that the members of the body – all of them – are wholly submissive to his word and example.

Compromises with the world

This extreme can be recognised because it is at the opposite end of the spectrum from the extreme that elevates law. It is not interested in definitions of truth, and even asks with Pilate, "What is truth?", as if it is beyond God's ability to reveal His truth to mankind, so that each individual must search out for him or herself what is true. This extreme constantly points out what is wrong with the body, and how it needs to be radically changed, as if the body belongs to its members and not to its Lord, who alone has the right to determine how it should act. In abandoning a rule-based approach, this extreme tends to abandon all discernment because – so it is alleged – all disciples should be non-judgmental. This extreme claims to give equal weight to everyone's viewpoint, but with one marked exception – the viewpoint of the Lord who is the head. The outcome is not the political machinations of those who are law-based, but it leads instead to anarchy. Decisions are not taken, as they were in the early ecclesias, following brotherly discussion among all members, but by individuals imposing their own solutions, irrespective of positions reached by their brothers and sisters after careful consideration around open Bibles and committed to the Father in prayer. Compromises are often made with the world, so as not to seem different or strange to those around. This extreme is content to trample on the consciences of fellow members, and ignores the apostles' warnings about the importance of having a conscience free from offence.

The table overleaf summarises the different ways various aspects of life in Christ can diverge from the high example he set.

More important than identifying these extremes is the task of learning from God's word how disciples should honour, respect and serve their head. The objective of these comments is not to point the finger of blame, but to acknowledge how easy it is to lose focus, and to encourage greater adherence to the Lord who is our head.

The Lord explained: "If you abide in my word, you are my disciples indeed. And you shall know the truth, and the truth shall make you free" (John 8:31,32). The significant point here is that disciples are asked *to*

11

Extremes that diverge from the headship of Christ		
	CHRIST THE HEAD	
What is truth?	Walking in the truth	*Truth is a formula of words*
Revolution	Transformation	*Conservation*
Licence	Principles	*Rules*
Anarchy	Brotherly dialogue	*Politics*
Peace at any price	Making peace & building unity	*First pure, then peaceable*
Open fellowship	Principled fellowship	*Restricted fellowship*
No traditions	Apostolic traditions	*Human traditions*
Holiness is wholly internal	Holiness from the heart	*External holiness*
Female liberation	Honouring God-given roles	*Male domination*

continue in Jesus' word. This must be the guiding principle both in their lives as individual disciples, and in the communal life of the body of Christ. Jesus' word, and how he continued in it throughout his lifetime, reveals God's truth to mankind. There can be no doubt about what is truth, as Pilate ought to have known, because it was evident in the innocent man who stood before him: in his demeanour, his attitude, his concern for others and his love of God.

Truth in daily life

For disciples, truth must be shown in the large and small things of daily life. Only in this way does the truth free them from worldly constraints. There is no bondage for the servant who, with open ears, listens attentively in order to serve his Lord for ever. No king, governor or magistrate can strike fear into the heart of the disciple who owns only Christ as Lord. There is no

12

task too great or service too small but it can reveal the principles that always guided the Christ-man.

The Lord's example, honestly followed, means that the needs of others – particularly those of fellow disciples – assume greater priority than those of self. If the Lord could walk through a country overcome and dominated by a foreign power without being tarnished or contaminated by lepers, law-makers, soldiers, grasping tax collectors or corrupt priests, his disciples too can manifest holiness without compromising their position, and in the process hold out the water of life to all who thirst after righteousness. The principle is simple, though its practice is hard: at every step, disciples should "serve the Lord Christ".

3

PRINCIPLES OF HEADSHIP

FOR schoolchildren, "the Head" is the Principal, the Head Teacher, Headmaster or Headmistress. The ultimate threat is to be sent to see the Head, who dispenses the appropriate discipline. He or she is the visible symbol of authority within the school, the embodiment of its ethos and the one who frames the rules. Heads are often feared, possibly respected, and occasionally loved. This is usually because those who hold the post seem remote and distant from the vast majority of their pupils; they are seen as figureheads rather than as individuals who lead real lives.

Head teachers have an enormous influence on their schools. Schools where there is generally good behaviour, and where pupils perform well in their studies and activities, usually have motivational head teachers. This is further emphasised by the fact that one of the key measures introduced to improve failing schools is a new head teacher who is expected to inspire and drive through the necessary changes.

The possibility of running a school without a head teacher is never contemplated. That would be a recipe for anarchy; authority would break down, and the environment for learning and growth would be destroyed.

The Lord Jesus Christ is the Head of the body of believers, and he has many similarities with the Head of a school. Believers learn through their association with him; they follow the curriculum he teaches, and are susceptible to the discipline of his commands. As Head of the ecclesia, he sets the tone, establishing an ethos which is distinctly associated with him.

14

A loving Saviour

The main similarities end there, however. The Lord Jesus does not inspire fear, but devotion and love. He should be respected, honoured and worshipped, for he is not remote, unapproachable or distant. It is very probable that unless there is a strong recognition of the Lord's living presence, he will *seem* remote, and more like a feared headmaster than a loving Saviour. Yet he wants and expects believers to develop a close personal relationship with him, and through him with other disciples.

The example of school life shows the importance of having a clear lead and a good leader. To be effective, members of a team need to know what is expected of them, and one of the main purposes of education is to help children fulfil their potential. Through his teaching staff, a headmaster tries to motivate pupils to develop their talents and make a positive contribution to society by means of their chosen career. Believers soon learn that their potential can only be fully realised in Christ and with his guidance; his authority must always be recognised, and also his concern for the whole ecclesia of God as well as for each individual brother and sister.

A fundamental moral truth

The leadership provided by the Lord is twofold. First of all, he expects nothing from his disciples that he has not done himself; he leads by example. And what an example it was, laying down his own life that others might enter with him into life eternal! Secondly, in developing true followers he establishes principles that have to be applied in many different situations. A principle can be defined as a fundamental moral truth that governs behaviour. We speak about a person of principle who makes a stand, sometimes at a high personal cost, in order to uphold the things he believes in. Principles differ from rules in a number of ways. Rules may be devised for expediency, and have nothing to do with upholding a principle. Rules tend to be proscriptive, stating what should *not* be done, whereas principles free individuals to do something that is worthwhile and honourable. One is negative and tends to produce resistance, the other is positive and liberating.

There is no doubt that the Lord Jesus led a highly principled life. The example he set was one where the factors that motivated his behaviour were clearly displayed for all to see. As he declared himself, he modelled his own behaviour on his Father's:

> "The Son can do nothing of himself, but what he sees the Father do; for whatever he does, the Son also does in like manner." (John 5:19)

He saw the character of his heavenly Father, who is merciful and gracious, longsuffering and abundant in goodness and truth, and patterned himself on what he saw. No wonder the Apostle John was able to write of Jesus that he was *"full* of grace and truth". Knowing that it was always his endeavour to manifest the Father's characteristics, Jesus exclaimed to Philip:

> "Have I been with you so long, and yet you have not known me, Philip? He who has seen me has seen the Father; so how can you say, 'Show us the Father'?" (John 14:9)

These characteristics form both the highest principles and the strongest foundation for life. 'Truth' translates into upright dealings between individuals in every sphere of human concourse: within families, in marriage, in business, in ecclesial life, and in general society. But truth by itself can sometimes be harsh, unyielding and unfeeling. As the saying has it, "truth hurts". In the Lord Jesus, therefore, as with his Father, truth was combined with grace, which comprises mercy, goodness and patience. It can be summed up in the wonderful scriptural term, "lovingkindness".

"By grace are ye saved"

Truth can be impersonal, formal and cold, but "grace and truth" cannot. Grace implies knowledge of the

16

person to whom it is extended, and it is an element in the relationship that can exist between individuals. So far as believers are concerned it is the primary factor in their relationship with the Lord Jesus Christ, "for by grace you have been saved through faith, and that not of yourselves; it is the gift of God, not of works, lest anyone should boast" (Ephesians 2:8,9).

The divine principles that were apparent in the life of the Lord are here contrasted with "works", by which the apostle means actions undertaken with a view to placing another individual under an obligation. A parent can agree, for example, to let his or her child have a special treat on condition that certain household chores are satisfactorily completed. The motivation for undertaking those chores is primarily the promised reward. While the child both loves and respects his parents, he tidies his room, sweeps the driveway or mows the lawn so that he can claim the reward: this becomes the major – and sometimes the only reason.

Principles are much more demanding. In the first place they demand greater maturity, so that it is difficult to convey them in words to a toddler, who is often better knowing the behaviour that is demanded of him by means of simple instructions: "do this; don't do that". Principles can be revealed in action much more effectively than it is possible to display or manifest rules. Someone who is described as a 'man of principle' does not spend all his time explaining that his actions flow from a creed he has determined to follow; his daily conduct declares much more loudly and clearly than words the principles by which he lives.

Deeply embedded

Just as a certain level of maturity is necessary to understand the concept of principles, their application is also dependent on a person's maturity. Principles have tentacles that reach deeply into an individual's life. They are not limited to actions, as Jesus declared when he explained the difference between a rule and a principle:

"You have heard that it was said to those of old,
'You shall not commit adultery.' But I say to you that
whoever looks at a woman to lust for her has already
committed adultery with her in his heart."

(Matthew 5:27,28)

Here, he showed how deeply principles must be
embedded so that they control unbidden thoughts, and
this cannot happen overnight.

Those who have been trying to follow the Lord
throughout a long life will testify how their behaviour
has been modified (and continues to be modified) by an
increasing awareness of the extent that divine
principles affect their lives. The person who once spoke
of "the university of life" revealed a great truth. We first
of all embrace divine truths as wonderful statements
about God's dealings with mankind in the past, His gift
of the Lord Jesus Christ through whom a way of
salvation was opened for sinful men and women, and
the great promises about God's kingdom on earth and
the restoration of all things. These truths all have
important moral consequences, so that we cannot
continue to live as we once lived in the times of our
ignorance. The response to the Gospel is made on a
daily basis in lives lived more in accordance with the
principles that motivated the Lord.

Giving divine principles their highest value

It is impossible to deny from the examples given by
Jesus during the Sermon on the Mount that principles
are far, far more demanding and exacting than rules.
And with the Lord's example of living by divine
principles, the highest possible standard has been set
for his disciples to follow. It is therefore possible to
recognise that a situation could develop where it is
accepted that believers should no longer live by rule-
based works, yet they fail to give godly principles their
true and highest value. Here the pendulum swings
strongly in the direction of "grace" and gives little or no
place for "truth". Like the school that has no direction
or head, the outcome is anarchy: where anything goes.

This is as far adrift from the position adopted by the Lord, as the situation that is controlled by law with its reliance on works. Neither approach allows its followers to develop truly Christ-like lives, and they both arise from failure properly to appreciate God's word as it has been revealed in the beautiful life of His Son.

When considering the principles that are revealed in the scriptures, we must always remember their source. They come from God: they are manifested in His ways, and were made flesh in His Son. As always, the Lord is our example. He is therefore supremely our Teacher, Master and Lord, and we are his disciples.

In the school of life, he is the Head, the Principal, and we are his students.

4

ONE BODY

THERE is one head, even Christ. Paul therefore informed the brothers and sisters at Corinth that Christ cannot be divided, by which he meant that one head cannot rule over a body that chooses to serve many different leaders. The presence of only one head demands that the body too must be one, giving rise to some important implications for those who are members of the body of the Lord Jesus Christ. A short passage in Hosea makes a useful starting point for a consideration of Bible teaching about this subject:

"The children of Judah and the children of Israel shall be gathered together, and appoint for themselves one head; and they shall come up out of the land, for great will be the day of Jezreel!"

(Hosea 1:11)

The prophet looked forward to the time when the promises to Abraham will be fulfilled and "the number of the children of Israel shall be as the sand of the sea". Under the leadership of one captain, those who are Abraham's seed will go out from the land to subdue all nations in the day when God visits the nations of the world for His holy name's sake. The image of soldiers in Christ's army powerfully confirms the message about one body. For in order to operate satisfactorily, an army must act unitedly, obeying implicitly the directions issued by its commanding officer.

One commander

In whatever part of the army individual soldiers may serve, they are joined together by virtue of the common aim which they all share. A divided body results from not having clear direction, or from rebellion within the ranks. In the Christ-body, there is no lack of clarity in the commands issued by the Master, so division occurs only because his commands prove unacceptable to some, or because they serve another commander despite claiming to serve Christ.

The Lord's intentions are clear. In his great intercessory prayer before his agony, Jesus on three occasions expressed his desire that his disciples "may be one" (John 17:11,21,22). He based this on his own unity with his Father, and prayed that his disciples "may be one in *us*", sharing that unity. He asked specifically that God would keep disciples in His name: i.e., as part of His glorious purpose whereby all the world will give Him honour and praise. Jesus had declared the glory he personally shared with God in such a way that he was able to tell Philip, "he who has seen me has seen the Father" (John 14:9). He wants his disciples to have the same closeness to the Father's word, and the same desire to do His will that he displayed throughout his mortal life.

The qualities of the Christ-body should thus be the ones revealed in God's name: mercy, grace, patience, abundant goodness and truth. Such characteristics bind individuals together, whereas divisions and schisms are caused when discord, jealousy, anger and malice are present.

Dividing the body

Other evidence of division in the Christ-body is apparent when groups of individuals or ecclesias develop around a particular approach to the truth, a style of worship, a special emphasis on one teaching or another, a magazine or perhaps a prominent brother. Such groups can quickly develop their own language and methods, and in the process intentionally or unintentionally start to separate themselves from the rest of the body. Taken to an extreme, groups start to communicate only with those whom they believe to be like-minded, so that details of gatherings and events

21

are not circulated for the benefit of all, but are sent only to selected recipients.

The effect of this is that the body of Christ is redefined, and those who become involved with one group or another are literally eccentric, because their centre is different from that recognised by the body of which they claim to be part. Over time, it becomes harder to correct the inevitable imbalance because the view of the true centre has grown unclear or become distorted. Though examples can be invidious, they are needed in order to appreciate the point being made. Some matters around which groups have formed – with the danger of dividing the body of Christ – include the style of our musical praise, the way in which our Heavenly Father is addressed, attitudes towards Bible prophecy, the role of sisters within the community, reactions to issues arising in marriage, views about the sacrifice of our Lord, etc. These are all subjects that can generate heat and emotion, and if unchecked can lead to separation or division.

Once a particular position is taken, usually one that more closely defines an issue, a process of polarisation commences. Others may be attracted to the stated position, reinforcing the differences and adding to the separation of the group from others in the body.

Perceiving the principles

This is not a new phenomenon. The apostles had to warn the early ecclesias against brethren who were more involved in detailed questioning than in "godly edification" (1 Timothy 1:4). The danger was also apparent in the early history of the brotherhood, and a warning was issued in the form of a landmark article entitled, *True Principles and Uncertain Details*. Brother Roberts' words benefit careful attention:

"So much of division is inevitable, and while lamenting it, men of God can but submit, with as little asperity towards those who cause it as possible. But there are divisions that are uncalled for, and therefore sinful. Paul refers to such when he says:

22

'Mark them that cause divisions among you contrary to the doctrine (the teaching on unity) that ye have learnt.' He was referring, no doubt, to the factions arising out of personal preferences, but the warning applies to all divisions that ought not to be made. There is division enough, in all conscience – division that is inevitable – division that must be, unless we are to ignore divine obligations altogether; but there are divisions that ought not to be. It is possible to go too far in our demands on fellow-believers. How far we ought to go and where to stop, is at one time or other a perplexing problem to most earnest minds. They are afraid on the one hand of compromising the truth in fellowship; and on the other, of sinning against the weaker members of the body of Christ. The only end there can be to this embarrassment is found in the discrimination between true principles and uncertain details that do not overthrow them.

"There are general principles as to which there can be no compromise: but there are also unrevealed applications of these principles in detail which cannot be determined with certainty, and which every man must be allowed to judge for himself without any challenge of his right to fellowship. To insist on uniformity of opinion on those uncertain details is an excess of zeal which may be forgiven, but which meanwhile inflicts harm and distress without just cause." (*The Christadelphian*, 1898, page 182)

Brother Roberts built on this introduction by giving examples of subjects where true principles can be lost by brethren insisting on uncertain details. The examples he cited were: the nature of God; the nature of man and of angels; the earth, sun, moon and stars; reigning with Christ; the devil; Moses; the resurrection call; immortality; the future temple; and the judgement seat and who will appear there. It is apparent from this list that almost any subject can be pressed to the point where brethren can be divided, introducing deep fissures into the body.

Drawing together

How can this outcome be prevented? One approach has already been mentioned – by greater concentration on our head, who is Christ. Too often imbalance occurs because individuals try to meet their own needs, or operate on the basis of what seems right to them. The touchstone must always be, What did the Lord say? How can we best serve and honour him? But there is something else as well. Alongside an emphasis on the head must be a concern for the body as a whole.

It is just as easy to concentrate on one aspect or one part of the brotherhood to the exclusion of all else as it is to press a subject or topic to an extreme and create a point of difference that can grow into a potential division. The needs of our own ecclesia can easily blind us to work in the wider brotherhood that desperately needs help and support. Alternatively, a brother or sister can become so immersed in the work of one of the organisations in the brotherhood that needs much nearer to home are completely overlooked.

Some brothers and sisters have special needs, and these often require special treatment. But wherever possible these needs should be met alongside, and not separate from the rest of the body. Sunday schools, for example, have always been seen as part of an ecclesia's work, and not as a separate entity. The same is true for youth activities: these should be organised in ways that encourage greater ecclesial involvement, rather than as occasions that separate young people from the activities of the rest of the body.

Different approaches to the various activities in the brotherhood may help to show why it is vital to have concern for the needs of *the whole body*. One extreme view is that many activities and events are insufficiently rigorous; the response is to choose not to attend, and to warn others of potential dangers. Another extreme view, particularly when criticisms are made, is to ignore completely any sensitivities that have been expressed, and carry on regardless. Neither of these approaches gives due consideration to the whole body of Christ. Neither shows the love of the brotherhood enjoined on all disciples by the Apostle Peter (1 Peter 2:17).

Keep in touch

Keeping in touch with all the various activities of the brotherhood is important. Brothers and sisters should take every opportunity to visit other ecclesias and join in activities that are arranged for the benefit of all. This can be in their own locality, and elsewhere – perhaps in conjunction with holidays or work-related travel. Information about the brotherhood is published in magazines that carry news from ecclesias all round the world. The reports help to build up a picture of what is happening, and encourage brothers and sisters to offer assistance and to include particular needs in their personal prayers.

The Lord was so concerned for the body that he laid down his life for it. There can be no greater example to mould our attitude towards our brethren and sisters. "We also ought to lay down our lives for the brethren" (1 John 3:16).

5

THE NEW CREATION

EVERY true disciple yearns for the day when the kingdom of God will be established on the earth, for "the whole creation groans and labours with birth pangs together until now ... waiting for the adoption, the redemption of our body" (Romans 8:22,23).

What will life in the kingdom be like for faithful believers, both in relation to the Lord and towards fellow disciples? Is it possible that some saints will refuse to carry out the Lord's wishes, or grumble behind his back? Could there be dissension in their ranks, or petty jealousies liable to develop into deep rifts that could shatter the fellowship they enjoy?

Such propositions are ludicrous; they are totally incompatible with the scriptural concepts of immortality and sanctification. Every prophecy of the kingdom leaves no doubt about the intimate bonds that will exist between disciples and their Lord, and with each other when they live and reign with him. Many of these prophecies are expressed symbolically, but are no less powerful for that reason. The book of Revelation, for example, opens with the Apostle John being granted a vision of the Christ-man of the future age – the Lord Jesus Christ and his glorified and faithful disciples, speaking with one heart and one voice, "as the sound of many waters" (Revelation 1:13-16). A few chapters later, in another vision, John sees Jesus enthroned in glory surrounded by an adoring multitude of saints symbolised by four living creatures and twenty-four elders. Their worship is pure and untarnished by dissent or disagreement: "You are worthy, O Lord, to receive glory and honour and power; for you created all

things, and by your will they exist and were created"
(4:11).

"The new man"

Jesus is the head of the new creation, and his body is
that "new creature", brought forth "by the word of
truth, that we might be a kind of firstfruits of his
creatures" (James 1:18). This new creation commenced
with the Lord's sacrifice, and new creatures are being
formed as men and women respond to the call of the
Gospel. They "put off, concerning your former conduct,
the old man which grows corrupt according to the
deceitful lusts, and ... put on the new man which was
created according to God, in true righteousness and
holiness" (Ephesians 4:22-24).

The "old man" is crucified with Christ, first of all
symbolically through association with the Lord's death
as men and women enter the waters of baptism, and
subsequently as disciples crucify the flesh with its
affections and lusts by treating human, earthy desires
as if they are completely dead and void of power
(Galatians 5:24; Colossians 3:5). In serving Christ, true
believers are no longer servants of sin: "our old man
was crucified with Christ, that the body of sin might be
done away with, that we should no longer be slaves of
sin" (Romans 6:6). The "new man" that is being formed
through this process is described in the most lofty terms
it is possible to use. Whereas Paul told the Ephesians
about the need to "put on the new man", he explained to
the Galatians that this was achieved when they "put on
Christ" (Galatians 3:27). Later, as he described his
personal anguish and concern on their behalf, he spoke
of the process continuing "until Christ is formed in you"
(4:19).

Members of his body

The visions of the kingdom, and the Apostle's
description of the new creation, show how our Heavenly
Father looks upon believers. In his sight, because they
are "in Christ", corporately they are one with him, and

27

can therefore be described appropriately as "Christ". While it is true that each individual disciple "puts on Christ", the process of growing up into Christ who is our head is particularly applicable to the whole community of believers, which will finally be "the perfect (i.e., mature, or full-grown) man" (Ephesians 4:13). Individuals grow into Christ as members of his body, and never by isolating themselves from the other members.

The close bond between disciples and their Lord in the kingdom, a bond that unites the saints in complete and harmonious service, is therefore reliant upon how we respond during our mortal probation, and particularly on the communal life shared with fellow believers. The new creation has already begun, and the process is at work now; it will not be complete until all the harvest of the kingdom is safely gathered in. It is inconceivable that any who shun the companionship of their brethren and sisters now, will miraculously wish to spend eternity in their company. As the previous chapter showed, holding the head demands that individual disciples also hold the body – all of it, and not just the parts that a person might be attracted to naturally.

Unity in the brotherhood

Is there in the brotherhood this sense of unity, deriving from the one whom we acknowledge as the Head? Do we see individual brethren and sisters working together, preaching together, praying together? Honesty compels us to admit that problems, disagreements and tensions often prevent the complete unity so many desire. Yet there are occasions and circumstances that always bring the brotherhood together as one, so that it is possible to glimpse something of the harmony that is apparent in scriptural descriptions of the future age.

When natural catastrophes or large-scale human tragedies occur, the welfare of brethren and sisters is uppermost in the minds of all who learn of the disaster. Earthquakes, floods, famines, wars and terrorist attacks all focus attention on the consequent human suffering, and the possibility that some members of the body of Christ may be inadvertently affected. The Apostle rightly commented, "If one member suffers, all the members suffer with it" (1 Corinthians 12:26). News of a tragic illness or personal disaster immediately creates a wellspring of sympathy, surrounding the suffering brother or sister with loving arms and much needed support. Long term disagreements or personal slights are quickly forgotten, because they pale into insignificance beside the enormity of a desperate tragedy.

Equally, if "one member is honoured, all the members rejoice with it". Information about how the truth of the Gospel is spreading in new lands, or the return of a long-lost brother or sister draws everyone together in a common bond of thankfulness and rejoicing.

Times of trial and persecution also have the same effect. Previous differences are soon put aside when attacks against the faith require that brothers and sisters stand shoulder to shoulder to defend the Truth against ridicule or unjust criticism. Conflict and oppression in the wider world often produce greater unity in the brotherhood.

Why is the unity that ought to exist between brothers and sisters only truly evident at such times? Why on most other occasions is there less emphasis on matters that draw believers together, and more emphasis on issues of secondary importance that can be allowed to create divisions and conflict? The obvious explanation is that too often brethren and sisters forget to follow the example of the Lord. Other things assume a greater importance so that they no longer think, act and speak as the Lord did. Christ is no longer "all and in all" (Colossians 3:11). Such situations mark a drift away from living directly under his leadership and influence; and if he is no longer the main influence in life, there must be another factor that for a time at least assumes a greater authority.

The influences that draw believers away from the Lord Jesus Christ are all related to "the old man". The effect is that the process of the new creation is halted, and the characteristics of the old man start once again to take precedence. The mind of the Lord is no longer the guiding force it should be, and attention is directed away from the spiritual needs of the body as a whole towards the natural needs of the individual disciple.

A warning from Corinth

The Apostle Paul, hearing of problems in Corinth, said: "when you come together as a church, I hear that there are divisions among you, and in part I believe it" (1 Corinthians 11:18). He appreciated that the formation of the new man in Christ is not straightforward, and that sometimes brothers and sisters slip backwards and fail to make the necessary progress. His next comment, however, is particularly important: "For there must also be factions among you, that those who are approved may be recognised among you" (verse 19).

Not everyone will be caught up by faction, debate and strife. Some brothers and sisters will show how the mind of Christ has developed in them, using their energies to build up, console, strengthen and draw together rather than tear apart. In Corinth when brothers and sisters met together to fulfil the Lord's command to "do this in remembrance of me", "each one takes his own supper ahead of others; and one is hungry and another is drunk" (verse 21). The deep divisions which Paul mentions at the start of his first letter to the Corinthian ecclesia were clearly reflected at the breaking of bread, where brothers and sisters were not truly coming together as one.

If one consequence of the existence of such factions is that "those who are genuine ... may be recognised" (verse 19, RSV), how could the Apostle describe the best way to respond to divisions, backbiting, and lack of unity? He drew attention to the highest example of all, explaining that "the Lord Jesus on the same night in which he was betrayed took bread; and when he had given thanks, he broke it and said, 'Take, eat; this is my body which is broken for you; do this in remembrance of me" (verses 23,24). The point he was making is that the last supper was held on "the night in which he was betrayed", when there was deep division among the disciples through Judas' defection. During supper, Jesus handed Judas the sop, a measure of how much Judas was loved. The Lord's action was an implicit appeal for the traitor to reconsider his plans. Jesus was impressing two important considerations upon Judas, if he was prepared to heed them. First, to rethink what he intended to do in regard to the Lord, and secondly to review his position among the disciples.

This was the background of Paul's words to the Corinthians. The existence of problems, divisions and factions will reveal those who are genuinely putting on Christ, and those who are reverting to the old man. Some, like Judas choose not to discern the Lord's body. Others, patterning their behaviour on the Lord Jesus will continue to try drawing back to the body all who are drifting from it. The Apostle made an urgent appeal that is not restricted to the first century ecclesia; it is just as relevant today: "let your coming together not be unto judgement".

6

IT SHALL BE ONE TABERNACLE

THE analogy used by the Apostle Paul whenever he writes about the headship of the Lord Jesus Christ is based on the human body, whose various parts all have different roles, yet are directed by the head, so that as an orchestra under the leadership of its conductor, a true harmony can be achieved. In the case of the Christ-body, the objective is to give glory to the God of Heaven. The details of this analogy are evident in the words that the apostle uses: head, body, joints, knit-together, etc. He speaks of the parts of the Christ-body *growing up* into the head, and thus of the whole body itself growing and increasing. This is true numerically, of course, for as each year passes the number of the elect increases, and will continue to increase until the body is complete and ready to be finally and irrevocably united with the head.

The idea of growth also refers to spiritual development, which must be the aim of all believers, and can only be achieved by remaining focused on the head and living in harmony with his example. This growth in the individual parts of the Christ-body is not independent of all the other parts, but is beneficially assisted by individuals being in fellowship one with another, so that the whole body builds up itself in love.

A body ... a building

What is not immediately obvious in the passage in Ephesians is the subtle change of analogy. Paul talks of believers who can "*grow up* in all things into him who is the head – Christ", and then of the consequences that flow from being associated with the Lord as the body "*edifying* (or building up) itself in love" (Ephesians

4:15,16). The first term – "grow up" – relates to natural things: plants, animals, people; the second term – "build up" – relates to man-made structures such as buildings. The apostle on other occasions in his letters makes the same smooth transition between metaphors. In 1 Corinthians 3:9, for example, he explains, "For we are God's fellow workers; you are God's field, you are God's building". Believers are both plants in the Father's vineyard, and stones in His temple. The owner of the vineyard is still looking for fruit, and the building is still under construction – both should be growing as they receive nourishment and direction from the head.

The Lord Jesus is therefore both the head of the body, and the headstone of the building, which "grows into a holy temple in the Lord" (Ephesians 2:21). The same honour attaches to the headstone as attaches to the head of a human body. The headstone crowns the completed building, which has to be set out right from the lowest foundation with reference to the position the headstone will finally occupy.

This was foreseen in a prophecy given at the time when God's people were returning to the land from captivity to rebuild the temple, and the prophet Zechariah's words contained a longer term message as well as encouragement to the people of his own day. He spoke of a time when in the purpose of God: "He shall bring forth the capstone with shouts of 'Grace, grace to it!'" (Zechariah 4:7). The apostles recognised that the fulfilment of this prophecy began with the sending of the Lord Jesus Christ, and will continue until the whole construction is finished. The Apostle John said of the Lord Jesus during his earthly ministry: "We beheld his glory, the glory as of the only begotten of the Father, full of grace and truth" (John 1:14); and many others will join with these sentiments when the Lord returns in glory at the completion of his Father's temple.

Fitly joined together
Once we recognise that the apostle is using a double analogy in Ephesians when he writes about "the head",

33

some further details also emerge. He writes about the various parts being "fitly joined together", and the importance of the joints and what they supply to this 'body-temple' he describes. Similar language appears also in Colossians, where Paul writes about those who fail to hold fast to "the Head, from whom all the body, nourished and knit together by joints and ligaments, grows with the increase that is from God" (Colossians 2:19). Why should Paul use this language? What would it mean to his readers? What message does it hold for us?

The outcome of the process he describes is "a holy temple in the Lord, in whom you also are being built together for a dwelling place of God in the Spirit" (Ephesians 2:21,22). Paul clearly bases his analogy on the occasion when God instructed Israel: "Let them make me a sanctuary, that I may dwell among them" (Exodus 25:8). The apostle is using tabernacle-language, and he directs his readers to compare the construction of a dwelling place of God by Israel in the wilderness of Sinai with the formation of the Christ-body by believers from all nations in the wilderness of the kingdom of men.

The inspired apostles were like Bezaleel and Aholiab who worked with the children of Israel to construct a building designed by God (Exodus 31:1-4). The Israelites had to bring offerings from which the tabernacle was eventually constructed, as if each willing-hearted individual was being built personally into the final edifice. This meant that the children of Israel were to recognise themselves in the different parts of the tabernacle structure: some as boards, some as poles, some as sockets or hooks, but all with a specific function.

Fellowship and unity

Viewed in this way, the tabernacle construction can be very fittingly applied to the growing spiritual temple described by the apostle. Some of the details of the tabernacle construction confirm the picture. Think, for example, of the boards made from acacia wood, and covered with gold, that formed the structure of the tabernacle. Each board was separate, yet had to become an integral part of the completed building. This was achieved by the presence of some special features. At the bottom of each board were "two tenons ... thus you shall make for all the boards of the tabernacle" (Exodus 26:17). These tenons were designed to slot neatly into silver sockets, which would hold the edge of one board tightly against the edge of its neighbour. The word for "tenons" is more usually translated "hands" (see KJV margin), which is particularly appropriate. The boards represented individual Israelites united together by standing in the presence of God hand in hand.

But how can a U-shaped line of tall boards be held together if they are connected only at the base? Foundations are important, of course, and the foundation of the spiritual temple is found in the teaching of "the apostles and prophets" (Ephesians 2:20). Yet something else was needed to keep the boards together. Two features are explained in Exodus 26. First was a system of horizontal bars that passed through rings set into the boards – what the apostle later describes as "knit together by joints and ligaments" (Colossians 2:19). Secondly, the corner boards were fixed firmly together: "they shall be coupled together at the bottom and they shall be coupled together at the top by one ring" (Exodus 26:24). Coupled beneath *and* coupled above. The top coupling was "the head", and all was brought together "unto one ring". These details express both fellowship and unity.

Coupled together in one

With this picture in mind, it is possible to read Exodus 26 again and see the great emphasis on fellowship in the pattern of the tabernacle God gave Israel through Moses. Notice first of all the number of times the word "couple" is used. The ten embroidered curtains were "coupled" together into two sets of five. These two sets were then fitted with loops, and golden clasps were used to "couple the curtains together". The word translated here as "coupled" (Hebrew, *chabar*) means 'to join or bind together', and occurs in Psalm 94:20, where it is translated "fellowship".

A consideration of the tabernacle structure also indicates the source of true fellowship in the Gospel, for from the way the curtains were positioned over the board walls of the tabernacle, the joint between the two sets of curtains was exactly over where the veil separated the Holy Place from the Most Holy Place. This veil, the apostle says in Hebrews, represents the Lord's humanity which was so necessary for our salvation (Hebrews 10:20). How appropriate that the coupling of the tabernacle should centre on the redeeming work of Christ, which binds all together in one!

The message in Exodus, provided for the benefit of "the ecclesia in the wilderness", is therefore the same as the one presented by the Apostle Paul to new ecclesias in Christ in the first century. Each individual believer should appreciate that he or she is called to be an integral part of the temple where God will be pleased to dwell. Their own will must submit to His, so that He alone is glorified. Though they are many, they become one in Him. This is expressed beautifully in Exodus 26 which describes how the different curtains are all assembled and coupled together so that it may "be one tabernacle" (verse 6).

That they may be one

The same point is made by the Lord when he considered God's purpose for his disciples, and it forms the theme of his wonderful high-priestly prayer in John 17:

"Holy Father, keep through your name those whom you have given me ... that they all may be one, as you, Father, are in me, and I in you; that they also may be one in us." (verses 11,21)

The Apostle Paul describes this wonderful unity as the "mystery of his (God's) will, according to his good pleasure which he purposed in himself, that in the dispensation of the fullness of the times he might gather together in one all things in Christ, both which are in heaven and which are on earth – in him" (Ephesians 1:9,10).

Believers today must show their desire to be wholly at one with the Lord when he comes, by holding fast to him now both individually and as constituent parts of a community of his disciples, for "we, being many, are one body in Christ, and individually members of one another" (Romans 12:5).

7

"HIGH AND LIFTED UP"

PREVIOUS chapters have stressed from passages
in the New Testament letters the importance of
acknowledging the headship of the Lord Jesus
Christ, but where is the subject of his headship first
found in the scriptures? The Apostle Paul uses the
metaphor throughout his writings, but he did not coin
it. He picked up the Lord's own words from John 12:32,
"And I, if I be lifted up from the earth, will draw all men
unto me".

Jesus was referring to an Old Testament teaching
about his mission, in which the necessity of his being
"lifted up" was described. The phrase refers specifically
to the twofold nature of the Saviour's work: his sacrifice
through which believers' sins can be forgiven, and his
glorification whereby men and women can have hope of
eternal life through him. Nor was it the only occasion
that John records the Lord talking of his being "lifted
up". In chapter 8, he reports Jesus' conversation with
the Jewish leaders who refused to acknowledge that he
was sent by God: "When you lift up the Son of man", he
said, "then you will know that I am he, and that I do
nothing of myself; but as my Father taught me, I speak
these things" (verse 28).

Earlier in his ministry, Jesus spoke to Nicodemus,
one of the Jewish leaders, whose curiosity drove him to
seek out the Lord during the hours of darkness. He
learned that his companions' vendetta against Jesus
was foretold through an incident in their nation's
history: "As Moses lifted up the serpent in the
wilderness, even so must the Son of man be lifted up,
that whoever believes in him should not perish but
have eternal life" (3:14,15).

Related to the Lord

In all these references, the Lord Jesus was speaking about his forthcoming death, explaining that it would be a critical incident to draw faithful men and women into association with him. Because it is vital to an understanding of his relationship to believers, and our relationship to him, it is worth following the line of thought the Lord introduced.

He started with the nation of Israel in the wilderness, when "the people spoke against God and against Moses: 'Why have you brought us up out of Egypt to die in the wilderness?'" (Numbers 21:5). In response to their lack of faith, God sent fiery serpents among them, and many people died from the serpents' bites. The serpents were probably described as "fiery" from the burning effect of the poison that led to the victim's death. It is hard to miss the appropriateness of what occurred. By failing to honour God or have respect for His care, the Israelites were following the ways of their father Adam. The serpents' bite was therefore like sin, whose poison – unless it is checked – leads unerringly to death. Paul confirms this in 1 Corinthians 15:56,57, where he says, "the sting of death is sin ... but thanks be to God, who gives us the victory through our Lord Jesus Christ".

He put away sin

The incident in the wilderness thus became an object lesson about how the sins of the world would be taken away in Christ. When the people asked Moses to pray for the removal of the serpents, God instructed him, "Make a fiery serpent, and set it on a pole; and it shall be, that everyone who is bitten, when he looks at it, shall live" (Numbers 21:8). On the basis of the Lord's own teaching, we are intended to see in the upraised serpent of bronze his own crucifixion when sin was dramatically conquered in one of Adam's race. All who look on the lifted-up Son of man can be cured of sin's sting of death. Of all Adam's many descendants, only Jesus nullified sin's poison by resisting all its urgings.

As the Apostle said, he "was in all points tempted as we are, yet without sin" (Hebrews 4:15).

In Numbers 21:8, when Moses was told to make "a fiery serpent", the emphasis is wholly upon the burning effect of the bite. Literally, the command was to make "a fiery (one)" (Hebrew, *saraph*); there is no word in this verse for "serpent". Displayed on the pole, and lifted up for all to see, was sin's power conquered and overcome. By the mercy of God, this victory was made available to all who lift their eyes realising that salvation can only come through the one man who destroyed "him who had the power of death" (Hebrews 2:14).

Every Israelite who faithfully looked up to the bronze serpent on the pole was cured of the serpent's bite; he shared in the benefit that it displayed – an antidote to the poisonous bite. By the power of God, he too was being drawn up from the ground where serpents make their home.

The glory of the Lord

This incident early in Israel's national history formed the backdrop to a vision granted to the prophet Isaiah "in the year that king Uzziah died" (Isaiah 6:1-7). John comments on this vision in his Gospel, explaining that Isaiah "saw his (i.e., Jesus') glory, and spoke of him" (John 12:41). Just as the incident of the serpent on a pole foreshadowed Jesus' crucifixion, so the vision granted to Isaiah revealed Jesus' glory.

So what did Isaiah see? He saw "the Lord sitting on a throne, high and lifted up, and his train of his robe filled the temple". The vision takes us beyond the crucifixion and shows the Son of man sitting "on the throne of his glory" (Matthew 25:31). Jesus is able to return to the earth in power and glory only because he first submitted to his Father's will by going obediently to the cross. As the Apostle Peter declared, "God raised (him) up, having loosed the pains of death, because it was not possible that he should be held by it" (Acts 2:24). The Spirit of Christ in the prophets therefore "testified beforehand the sufferings of Christ *and the glories that would follow*" (1 Peter 1:11).

In Isaiah's vision, however, the Lord was not alone. The train of his robe filled the temple, and lifted up with him were "seraphim", literally "fiery (ones)", clearly referring back to the "fiery (serpent)" of Numbers 21:8. The prophet immediately understood what the vision taught. He saw the immortal Lord in glory, high and lifted up through his conquering of sin; he also saw those who share his victory, and who will live and reign with him in glory. The effect on Isaiah was a deep sense of personal and national inadequacy: "I am a man of unclean lips, and I dwell in the midst of a people of unclean lips" (Isaiah 6:5). Continuing the figure that commenced with Israel in the wilderness being cured of the serpent's bite, fire in the form of a live coal was laid on the prophet's mouth and he was given the reassuring message: "your iniquity is taken away, and your sin purged" (verse 7).

These words contained the implicit promise that Isaiah too would be "lifted up" with the king when he returns in glory. If he, like the Israelites in the wilderness, looked to the salvation provided by God, and was drawn to be associated with him, he would be lifted from the effects of being descended from the man of the earth and enter into the joys brought by the man from heaven.

Seek things above

With this important background to the Lord's words, it is easier to see why the Apostle places so much emphasis upon holding to the head. For those who died with Christ in baptism, Paul had a special message which springs to life when viewed as an echo of Old Testament teaching in Numbers 21 and Isaiah 6:

"If then you were raised with Christ, *seek those things which are above*, where Christ is, sitting at the right hand of God. Set your mind on things above, not on things on the earth … When Christ who is our life

41

appears, then you also will appear with him in glory."
(Colossians 3:1-4)

Hope of living and reigning with Christ when he returns is therefore conditional on our association with him now. Though we can deny him, he remains faithful, and what he achieved continues to be powerful and able to draw men and women to him. Like Isaiah, with the eye of faith we can see him high and lifted up in glory, knowing that the vision of his glorious return could not be fulfilled without his first having been lifted up, like a bronze serpent, to destroy the power of sin. He will return in glory only because he first glorified his Father, putting aside his own natural desires and doing what had been planned before the foundation of the world.

An anchor of the soul

If we sincerely believe that sin could only be truly conquered in one of Adam's race who suffered all the effects of Adam's transgression, yet remained faithful at all times to God's will; and if this gives us hope of his imminent return in glory to bring the world into subjection to his Father's rule, then we must live now as if every part of life is centred on him. In the midst of a world bent on pleasure, with no thought of the consequences, true hope is found only in the Lord, high and lifted up. Christ alone is "the head". This hope set before us is "an anchor of the soul, both sure and steadfast", bringing with it "strong consolation" (Hebrews 6:18,19).

8

REALITY IS FOUND IN CHRIST

THE need for believers regularly to assess where they stand in relation to the Lord Jesus, who is their Head, has been discussed in the foregoing chapters mainly because of comments included in two of the letters of the Apostle Paul. He taught the necessity of self-examination in order that the problems besetting the early ecclesias could be quickly remedied. As disciples of the Lord Jesus, we pass through the wilderness of life needing both a handbook and a guide, and God has provided these in His word and His Son. Truly to know where we are and where we must go, we must take cross-bearings from a reliable point. That point is our Head.

The Apostle gave this advice particularly in two of his letters – the ones he wrote to believers in the ecclesias in Ephesus and Colosse. He explained that Jesus is "the head of the body, the church" (Colossians 1:18), and that this is no passive position, for he is "the head of the church; *and* he is the saviour of the body" (Ephesians 5:23). He is the saviour of the body because of what he accomplished in his triumphant victory over sin, and because he continues to lead disciples through the storms of life.

It is worth enquiring why this message was especially appropriate for brothers and sisters in Ephesus and Colosse. If it was necessary to point out to these two ecclesias the importance of holding to the person and example of Christ, what circumstances had occurred in Ephesus and Colosse that caused them to lose their focus on him? Are there lessons here for individuals and ecclesias in the twenty-first century?

43

A great metropolis

Both Ephesus and Colosse were cities in the Roman province of Asia. Ephesus particularly held a prominent position: it was the provincial capital, and was known as the first and greatest metropolis of Asia. The ecclesia was established by the Apostle Paul, and his preaching was so successful that many in the city abandoned their previous superstitious beliefs, making a great bonfire of their magical books. After two years, the impact of his preaching was felt by those in the city who profited from merchandise produced in association with the idolatrous worship of Artemis, or Diana of the Ephesians, and they were determined to rid themselves of him. Paul was saved from the riotous crowd by the timely intervention of the town clerk.

By contrast, the Apostle did not directly found the ecclesia in Colosse. He said in his letter that his readers there "have not seen my face in the flesh" (Colossians 2:1). Colosse was inland from Ephesus, on the road running east-west to Ephesus from the Euphrates to Rome, and it appears that brothers from Ephesus took the Gospel message there and an ecclesia was quickly established both in Colosse and in the surrounding towns like Laodicea and Hierapolis.

False teachers

The two ecclesias developed in different ways, through first falling prey to a similar problem. False teaching troubled them both. Paul warned the elders of Ephesus:

"After my departure savage wolves will come in among you, not sparing the flock. Also from among yourselves men will rise up, speaking perverse things, to draw away the disciples after themselves."
(Acts 20:29,30)

In Colosse, Paul was aware that his brothers and sisters were hearing "persuasive words", and were being beguiled by them (Colossians 2:4). They were being taught according to "the tradition of men", characterised as "philosophy and empty deceit" (verse 8).

44

The effect of this false teaching was different in the two cities. In both places it led directly to a wrong way of life, but in Ephesus it led to immorality, while in Colosse it led to a severe and self-denying austerity that became an end in itself, not achieving what it claimed. Both ecclesias were losing sight of their calling, and were no longer taking their bearings from the Lord who was their Head and their Saviour.

Though both epistles have something to say about the relationship between husbands and wives, parents and children, servants and masters, the treatment of these subjects in Ephesians suggests that the sanctity of marriage, obedience to parents and the humanitarian treatment of servants were not being upheld. It is probable that the general way of life in Ephesus, a leading imperial city devoted to the immoral worship of Artemis, sapped the moral fibre of brothers and sisters causing them to look more to their own personal pleasure and fulfilment than to the Lord and the needs of his ecclesia.

Human traditions

By contrast, the Colossians were being troubled by some who imposed external tests of righteousness – "do not touch, do not taste, do not handle" – as if such restrictions produce godliness. The Apostle called them "commandments and doctrines of men" (Colossians 2:21,22).

Both ecclesias had lost sight of the Lord Jesus Christ, and desperately needed to restore their equilibrium. Though the false teachings drove the two ecclesias to opposite extremes, the remedy was the same: to restore their focus on the Lord. A comparison of the two epistles reveals the enormous similarities between them (see table overleaf). The outcome of false teaching was radically different, but the Apostle's advice was effectively the same.

To drive home the importance of his message, Paul used a further weapon in addition to his call for the

Parallel passages in the two epistles	
Ephesians	**Colossians**
1:10	1:20
2:1,5	2:12,13
3:2	1:25
4:2-4	3:12-15
4:16	2:19
4:22-25	3:9,10
4:32	3:13
5:6-8	3:6-8
5:15,16	4:5
5:19	3:16
5:20-22	3:17,18
5:21 – 6:9	3:18 – 4:1
6:19,20	4:3,4
6:22	4:8

brothers and sisters to restore their focus on Christ. At the end of his letter to the Colossians, he wrote:

"When this epistle is read among you, see that it is read also in the church of the Laodiceans, and that you likewise read the epistle from Laodicea." (4:16)

It has been suggested that the Laodicean epistle is none other than what we know as the epistle to the Ephesians, and that it had wide circulation among the ecclesias in Asia Minor that were established by the work of brethren from Ephesus.* If this is so, then the two epistles are to be regarded as twin testaments to the Apostle's message. There is also evidence pointing to them being written at the same time, and delivered by the same messengers.

For those who were elevating human tradition and external observances, the remedy was to look to their Head, the Lord Jesus, "who is the beginning, the firstborn from the dead, that in all things he may have the preeminence" (1:18). The Colossians' problem arose

---

* Brother T J Barling, *The Letter to the Colossians*, pages 43-45.

because of the failure to elevate the Lord to the position given him by his Father. For those who tended to the opposite extreme, shunning anything they could characterise as legalistic and full of human tradition, the remedy was the same: to turn back to the Lord, remembering that God "hath raised us up with him, and made us sit with him in the heavenly places" (Ephesians 2:6, RV).

Opposite extremes

As these are extremes to which individuals and ecclesias can easily be drawn in modern times, the warnings and remedies are extremely timely. It must be noted that the two different ways of life arose directly from wrong teaching about the Gospel. In Colosse were brethren who placed a wrong emphasis, and who drew wrong conclusions about the importance of the law. They focused on that and failed to understand the power of the life and death of the Lord Jesus Christ. Paul countered this by his breathtaking descriptions of the centrality and exaltation of the Lord. One commentator has written about "the cosmic significance of Christ in Colossians",* for "he is before all things [i.e., even the law], and in him all things consist" (Colossians 1:17).

In Ephesus and other ecclesias in Asia Minor, like Laodicea, were brethren who taught only about the liberty we have in Christ Jesus as if individuals have freedom to ignore their brothers and sisters, and even some of the Lord's teachings, if they feel uncomfortable. The Apostle Paul showed those who went to this extreme that the Lord Jesus Christ is the Head of the Body. Though salvation is an individual matter, the needs and concerns of the whole ecclesia of Christ should be uppermost in the minds of disciples. Ephesians therefore deals with "the cosmic place of the Church",* i.e., the exalted place of believers who are related to heavenly things in Christ Jesus.

* *Ephesians*, by Francis Foulkes, Tyndale Commentries IVP, Page 32

Though the two letters contain the same advice – to look always to the Head, who is Christ – both must be read in order to strike the right balance between two extremes. One extreme upholding outward forms as if these produce holiness; and the other casting off moral restraint to uphold individual liberty. It is almost inevitable that a reaction to one extreme will result in a person (or an ecclesia) moving towards an opposite extreme. The extremes that were countered in the twin letters to Ephesus and Colosse can only be overcome by recognising them both as serious and potentially disastrous departures from the Gospel of Christ, and anyone adopting such positions as being not truly in him.

The Apostle therefore wrote to the brothers and sisters in Colosse, and said that "the reality" (as opposed to what they were being taught), "is found in Christ" (2:17, NIV). This is a message to be learned by each new generation.

9

THE WHOLE COUNSEL OF GOD

IN the previous chapter a comparison was made between the situation in first century Ephesus and Colosse, where both ecclesias were affected by individuals teaching things that were not wholly in accordance with the Gospel of Christ. In Ephesus, there arose a movement that caused the brothers and sisters to be diverted from the pathway to the kingdom. Their teachers sought disciples who would follow them, rather than directing the members of the ecclesia to follow one Master who is Christ, and this resulted in worldliness and libertarianism. In Colosse, the emphasis on commandments and doctrines of men created a dependence on laws, rules and regulations as the means of showing godliness, and in the process brothers and sisters became less like the Lord they claimed to follow.

Where did it all go wrong? Only a comparatively few years had passed since the Lord's death and resurrection, and most of the apostles were still alive, able to give eyewitness accounts of the Lord's teaching, his miraculous works and his character. They received the spirit of truth so that the message they taught came from accurate and inspired recollections of all they saw and heard when they were with him. The problem cannot have occurred through the failure of the apostles faithfully to represent the Gospel message, but lay with those who claimed to teach the Gospel they had received.

A reliable record
This contains an important lesson for disciples today. We no longer have the authoritative presence of the

apostles, but we do have their words recorded in the scriptures; these reveal the teaching of the Lord and give reliable accounts of his life, death and resurrection. There is clearly a great need, in view of the dangers that affected Ephesus and Colosse, to preach that message faithfully and completely, both to those who have not yet learned Christ, and within ecclesias to encourage brothers and sisters to remain true to their calling. Significantly, it was to the elders of the ecclesia at Ephesus that the Apostle Paul declared, "I did not shrink from declaring to you the whole purpose of God" (Acts 20:27, NASB).

There should be no surprise therefore that both individuals and ecclesias can become eccentric – i.e., not truly centred on their head, who is the Lord – if the message they regularly hear is partial and incomplete. One of the great advantages of following a daily Bible reading plan like *The Bible Companion* is that we are led through passages of scripture we might not otherwise choose to read. Some brothers and sisters claim not to find *The Bible Companion* helpful, but they will be seriously disadvantaged unless it is replaced by another method that also leads them systematically through "the whole purpose of God" – Old Testament and New Testament. The Law, the Psalms, the Prophets, the history of Israel, the Gospels and the Letters have all been recorded for our instruction, "that the man of God may be complete, thoroughly equipped for every good work" (2 Timothy 3:17).

Balanced programmes

Equally, it is possible that the message heard from our platforms is partial rather than complete. Brothers and sisters who attend only to break bread will not hear Bible classes or public lectures, and may not therefore be reminded of some of the fundamental aspects of our faith and how they are revealed by different means throughout the scriptures. But even for those who attend on every possible occasion, unless programmes are carefully prepared, the full range of God's purpose may not be directly addressed. Ecclesias should always seek to ensure that there is a balance in the Bible Class programme between subjects drawn from Old and New Testaments. With our public lectures, are all the first principles of the faith adequately and regularly presented?

We cannot hope to focus properly on our Head, unless we first know *about* him so that we might come to know him and love him. No wonder the Apostle Paul wrote to the brothers and sisters in Corinth, "I determined not to know anything among you except Jesus Christ and him crucified" (1 Corinthians 2:2). Every part of Bible teaching rests on the purpose of God in Christ; this is why the words of the prophets have been preserved and recorded. The Old Testament message is incomplete without its fulfilment in Christ, and the New Testament record cannot be fully appreciated without knowing the Old Testament background. It is certainly not insignificant that the New Testament opens by recording "the genealogy of Jesus Christ, the son of David, the son of Abraham" (Matthew 1:1), directing readers to the information recorded about these great men of faith.

The work of evil men

There is a further potential danger, where different aspects of Bible teaching are addressed in eccentric ways. Consider, by way of example, the subject of the crucifixion of the Lord Jesus Christ, the core message that Paul determined to preach in Corinth. It would be possible to look at this subject by concentrating on the evil minds of those who perpetrated the crime. The Lord's goodness was such, and his teaching so challenging that the Jewish leaders decided he must be silenced. Caiaphas believed it was expedient "that one man should die for the people, and not that the whole nation should perish" (John 11:50), and he did not shrink from encouraging the Jew's Council to find Jesus "deserving of death" (Matthew 26:66). They took him to Pilate and ensured that the threat of making himself

51

unpopular in the eyes of Caesar would drive Pilate to sanction Jesus' execution. On the day of Pentecost, Peter accused the Jews of killing the Lord: "You, with the help of wicked men, put him to death by nailing him to the cross" (Acts 2:23, NIV). This is in harmony with Psalm 2, where it was prophesied: "the kings of the earth set themselves, and the rulers take counsel together, against the LORD, and against his anointed" (verse 2); and the apostles quoted this Psalm after the same rulers tried to silence them just as they had silenced the Lord (Acts 4:26).

All this is true. But to concentrate only on the wicked deeds of those who opposed the Lord's teaching is not being faithful to all that the scriptures reveal about the circumstances of Christ's death. In the same breath as he accused the Jews of the death of Jesus, Peter explained that these things occurred because of "the determined purpose and foreknowledge of God" (Acts 2:23). We would be wrong therefore to talk about "Jesus Christ and him crucified" as if Peter's declaration had never been revealed. Nor is it just the case that an omniscient God foresaw what would happen when sinful man was confronted by the sinless Son of God. Peter did not say only that Jesus was delivered in accordance with God's foreknowledge of what wicked men would do to His Son, but that the crucifixion occurred as a result of His "determined purpose".

The slain lamb

This, of course, is the sense in which Jesus was "the Lamb slain from the foundation of the world" (Revelation 13:8), and how in his crucifixion, "God was in Christ reconciling the world to himself" (2 Corinthians 5:19). Despite these clear indications that the event was part of God's purpose from the beginning, many commentators have difficulty squaring the information with their preconceptions about a loving deity. Flying in the face of the whole counsel of God, they sometimes conclude that God did not send His Son with the purpose or aim to die for us; that it was all a tragic accident, yet foreseen by God and utilised by Him as an example of selfless obedience.

Here is the danger of not holding fast to the Head in what has been revealed about him. How can we know and love him without truly knowing *about* him? The only source of information on this subject is what is contained within the pages of our Bibles – the whole counsel of God.

Similar errors can arise by placing undue emphasis on Old Testament types and shadows, and not taking into account the fact that "the substance (or the reality) is of Christ" (Colossians 2:17). A very helpful comment on this subject occurs in Brother Fred Barling's, *Jesus – Healer & Teacher*. Writing of an Old Testament prophecy about the future work of Elijah, he says:

"With the assistance of the New Testament the full significance of these facts emerges; and, in turn, a careful re-reading of the Old helps towards the proper understanding of what is to some extent obscure in the New." (page 30)

This comment about the mutual interdependency of scriptures written before and after the coming of the Lord Jesus Christ provides a good guide to follow in all aspects of Bible teaching. Each aspect has its part to play, and we do a disservice to the inspired word if we neglect one part at the expense of another.

The fuller picture

An enormous privilege is granted to those who come to learn about God's work in Christ. Each piece of information is important towards filling out a more three-dimensional picture of what was achieved on our behalf. Commenting on his own inspired contribution to the material that describes the work of the Lord, the Gospel writer John explained that, "these are written that you may believe that Jesus is the Christ, the Son of God, and that believing you may have life in his name" (John 20:31).

10

TAKING HOLD

THE Apostle Paul explained how when preaching to the Corinthians he resolved to focus completely and exclusively on the Lord Jesus Christ and his work: "I determined not to know anything among you except Jesus Christ and him crucified" (1 Corinthians 2:2). This caused him not to show partiality towards any of his brothers and sisters, for it could be said even of the most awkward individual that he (or she) was also one "for whom Christ died" (8:11). He thus showed that a true appreciation of the Lord's work must affect the outlook and behaviour of all believers, especially – though not exclusively – towards fellow believers. When writing to brothers and sisters in Rome he therefore warned them: "Do not destroy ... the one for whom Christ died" (Romans 14:15).

We considered in the previous chapter the importance of giving proper weight to all the information provided in the scriptures about the Lord Jesus. This is particularly true when it comes to Bible teaching about his work of salvation. Many who claim to be followers of the Lord ignore some of the critical details given in God's word. Orthodox views in most of the churches of Christendom, for example, concentrate almost wholly on Jesus' unity with his Father, and in the process filter out the implications of the passages that explain how he shared our common humanity. The effect of this view is that the Lord Jesus is distanced from mankind, surrounded by a mystic aura and with little impact on the affairs of daily life.

The trouble with a distorted emphasis is that in restoring the balance there is always a danger of going too far in the opposite direction, and there is great need for care lest when we explain that the Lord was "in all points tempted as we are, yet without sin" (Hebrews 4:15), we somehow fail also to give due place to the comment that he was by angelic proclamation "that holy one ... the Son of God" (Luke 1:35). There should be no surprise, therefore, that in the scriptures almost every description of the Lord is quickly balanced by another. The Apostle's comment in Hebrews, for example, to which we have just referred contains two parts: first, he was tempted in every way as we are; and secondly, he never sinned. Thus he was like us, but he was also very different from us; he was a totally unique human being.

Choosing to suffer affliction

The truth about the Lord has to take account of both these aspects, and without giving both their true weight we shall not properly appreciate him or his work. Another example shows how important this principle is. In 2 Corinthians 8 the Apostle Paul was encouraging his readers to be generous in assisting their poverty-stricken brothers and sisters in Judaea. He suggested that they should emulate the Lord's example: "For you know the grace of our Lord Jesus Christ, that though he was rich, yet for your sakes he became poor, that you through his poverty might become rich" (verse 9). He was rich, yet he was poor. In any other circumstance this paradox would make no sense, but in the case of the Lord we know exactly what it means. With everything promised to him, Jesus voluntarily chose to identify himself with those he came to save. He could have grasped power, riches and might, but decided instead to share these with his friends in the day his Father has appointed when he will judge the world in righteousness. Like Moses who chose "rather to suffer affliction with the people of God than to enjoy the passing pleasures of sin" (Hebrews 11:25), he was looking to the recompense of the promised reward.

Though he had the ability instantly to gratify any human desire, Jesus chose instead to endure the ill-treatment experienced by his fellow-man. Like us he grew tired and was hungry, he could feel pain and sorrow, was able to laugh and cry. He matured and grew older, and he felt the strong pull of temptation described by the Apostle John as "the lust of the flesh, the lust of the eyes, and the pride of life" (1 John 2:16). Yet none of this should obscure the fact announced by the voice that came from heaven, "This is my beloved Son, in whom I am well pleased" (Matthew 3:17).

The path of life willingly accepted by the Lord, however, involved far more than sharing the common aspects of humanity mentioned above. Whereas it would have been possible for him as the Son of God to pass through life virtually untouched by the serious difficulties that beset many individuals, from the outset of his ministry Jesus made it abundantly plain that he would suffer undeserved ill-treatment at the hands of his fellow-men, and he refused to use his God-given powers for his own personal benefit. Did he not say about his symbolic death in the waters of Jordan, "thus it is fitting for us to fulfill all righteousness" (3:15)? The outcome of his life's purpose was wholly dependent on his willing submission to his Father's plan. As a member of the human race, the Lord's own deliverance from all the effects of humanity depended on his acceptance of the path of life of "the Lamb of God who takes away the sin of the world" (John 1:29).

He took hold of Abraham's seed

The phrase coined in the early years of the brotherhood to harmonise all the scriptural accounts of Jesus' work of salvation is that he did these things "for himself, that it might be for us" (*The Christadelphian*, March 1875, page 139). Whenever questions have been raised about the nature of the Lord's work, the danger of separating him from those he came to save has been highlighted. He must only be considered in the context of saving men and women from sin and death. As he said himself, "for this purpose I came to this hour" (John 12:27).

The Apostle in Hebrews therefore shows that, though Jesus was Son of God, he did not "give aid to", or "take hold of" (A.V., Greek, *epilambanomai*) angels, in the sense of sharing the angelic nature. No, he "took hold of" the seed of Abraham: "in all things he had to be made like his brethren, that he might be a merciful and faithful high priest in things pertaining to God, to make propitiation for the sins of the people" (Hebrews 2:16,17). There was no other way. The Saviour had to be one who completely shared our humanity, but who never gave way to its impulses. The work was therefore "for us", but it intimately involved the one sent to be our Saviour. He was not outside man's situation and requirements, but totally involved in them. And he was there by God's appointment, for "God was in Christ reconciling the world to himself" (2 Corinthians 5:19).

In the short article referred to above, Brother Roberts used the following helpful analogy:

"Supposing the case were leprosy instead of sin, and the cure to be passing through fire instead of death; but that the fire should only possess the power of cure where the disease existed without the virus of the disease, and that in all other cases the effect of the fire should be to destroy. Let the leprosy be death in the constitution, brought about by sin, and the virus, actual sin itself. By this illustration, all mankind are under the power of leprosy, which cannot be cured by the fire, owing to the presence of the combustible virus, which will catch fire and destroy the patient. If only one could be found free from the virus, he could go through the fire and save the rest: but he cannot be found. God interposes and produces such an one among them, one in whom the leprosy exists without the virus, that the rest may be cured by joining hands with him after he has gone through the fire. He goes through the fire 'for them'; but is it not obvious that he goes through it for

57

himself in the first instance? For if he is not delivered from the leprosy first, how will his going through the fire avail them? It is 'for himself that it might be for them'."

He took on him the form of a servant

Jesus was thus provided by God to answer the needs of sinful mankind; and these needs could not have been met satisfactorily by any other means. Whenever we read of what was done on our behalf, we should express deep thankfulness that the Lord "made himself of no reputation, taking (Greek, *lambano*, the root of the word used in Hebrews 2:16) the form of a bondservant, and coming in the likeness of men" (Philippians 2:7). While it is true that Jesus was amongst men as one who serves (Luke 22:27), this passage teaches that his service was always in the context of the conditions in which he found himself. He was a servant of the mortality he bore, though he was never mastered by it. This was the marvel of the Lord's life, and we wonder how it was possible for him to resist every temptation and remain spotless from sin. No wonder men and women fell at his feet during his earthly ministry and worshipped him. We should do no less, for he is deserving of the highest honour.

In the analogy set out above, mankind can only be cured from the leprosy of death and immunised against the virus of sin by joining hands with the Victor. As Jesus took hold of us, rather than of angels, so we must take hold of him, realising what has been achieved by him on our behalf. In identifying with the Lord's death and resurrection in baptism, and by sharing the emblems of his body and blood in fellowship, we acknowledge that in all things he was made like us, so that his Father's glory might be shown in his work of saving men and women from sin and death.

There are certain implications for all who hold to the Lord Jesus Christ. As he was made like us, we must strive to be like him. As noted at the beginning of this chapter, believers are to emulate Jesus by sacrificing

58

their time and energy to help fellow-believers. But it goes further than this: we are to try and live as he lived, think as he thought, resist temptations by using the scriptures he used, and display the divine attributes that we pray will be fully ours when mortality is swallowed up by eternal life.

Beliefs should become evident in the behaviour of Christ's disciples. Knowing that sins can be forgiven does not give license to keep on sinning that grace may abound. To act in this way is to let our hand slip out of the Lord's. Three times in the letter to the Hebrews, the apostle urges his readers to hold fast to God's purpose in Christ, without wavering: "Hold fast the confidence and the rejoicing of the hope firm to the end" (3:6). "Let us hold fast our confession" (4:14). "Let us hold fast the confession of our hope without wavering, for he who has promised is faithful" (10:23). Only by holding fast can the promises be fulfilled in us as they were in him.

11

THE COMFORTER

THE disciples could not accept the Lord's message when he spoke of leaving them to be with his Father in heaven. Sometimes he told them plainly, as when he said: "I am going away, and you will seek me, and will die in your sin. Where I go you cannot come" (John 8:21). On other occasions, he used parables like the one of the nobleman who "went into a far country to receive for himself a kingdom" (Luke 19:12). The information was particularly unpalatable because it was linked with the prediction of his approaching death in Jerusalem: "Jesus began to show to his disciples that he must go to Jerusalem, and suffer many things from the elders and chief priests and scribes, and be killed, and be raised the third day" (Matthew 16:21).

Despite the many times and different ways they were informed that the Lord would leave them to go into heaven, the disciples seemed painfully unprepared for the event. Their dejection is apparent in the demeanour of the two on the road to Emmaus, and even after all the Lord's appearances after his resurrection and his ascension into heaven, in the behaviour of the twelve as they hid away from public view. They were devastated by the Lord's absence, feeling alone, bereft and highly vulnerable.

It had been no different during his ministry when, for one reason or another, they were separated from him. In the storm-tossed boat on Galilee after the feeding of the five thousand, they were "straining at rowing, for the wind was against them", but felt the benefit of his presence as soon as he joined them, and "the wind ceased" (Mark 6:45-52). The disciples who did not witness Jesus' transfiguration failed to cure the epileptic boy, though the Lord "rebuked the demon" as soon as he returned to them, "and the child was cured from that very hour" (Matthew 17:14-18).

"I will come to you"

His absences exposed their vulnerability and weakness. How would they manage on his departure to heaven? "Because I have said these things to you, sorrow has filled your heart" (John 16:6). Jesus tried to prepare them, and strengthen them, by making an amazing promise. "I will not leave you orphans; I will come to you" (14:18). Just as he came to them miraculously over the Sea of Galilee, walking on the water, even so – despite his physical absence in heaven – Jesus assured his disciples that they would not be left on their own like fatherless orphans. His help would still be available: "whatever you ask in my name, that will I do, that the Father may be glorified in the Son" (verse 13).

By one of those wonderful spiritual paradoxes so beloved of John in his Gospel, it was necessary for the Lord to leave them, so that he could be with them – and with all who would believe on him through their work – for ever!

The passages in John's Gospel where this promise is explained in terms of the Comforter often leave us distinctly uncomfortable! It is difficult to read them without bringing to mind also what many professing Christians claim they mean, with their beliefs of an indwelling spirit guiding and directing the hearts of believers. But removing this preconception also removes all the difficulties it creates. Jesus' words are very appropriate to the needs of the disciples as we have discussed them. In simple terms, Jesus was promising his disciples that they could be as aware of his presence after his ascension as they were when he was physically with them. Did his physical absence mean that God's care for them was any less than when they walked beside him during his ministry? Of course not. Would his Father still hear and answer their prayers? Certainly, because they could now speak to

God in prayer as previously they had spoken to the Lord face to face.

"He ever liveth"

There was also an associated reassurance, in that the Lord promised he would be personally involved in their prayers and in responding to them: "If you ask anything in my name, I will do it", he said (John 14:14). This is confirmed in the Apostle's words in Hebrews, where he explains the enormous benefits to believers of the Lord opening up a way of access to the Father: "Let us therefore come boldly to the throne of grace, that we may obtain mercy and find grace to help in time of need" (Hebrews 4:16). None of this would have been possible without the resurrection and glorification of the Lord, "therefore he is also able to save to the uttermost those who come to God through him, since he always lives to make intercession for them" (7:25).

Whenever this reassurance is given it always contains an important qualification, emphasising that believers are not left on their own. It is not simply that the Lord has opened up a way of access to the Father for his disciples, but that he continues to be intimately involved on their behalf. They approach the Father in prayer *in his name*; they "come to God *through him*". Or as the Apostle John writes, "We have an advocate (Greek, *parakletos*) with the Father, Jesus Christ the righteous" (1 John 2:1). "Advocate" in this passage translates the same word that Jesus used to describe how the disciples would not be left as orphans; they would have a "Comforter" (*parakletos*). The word suggests the presence alongside of help and succour – exactly what the disciples feared might not be true when the Lord left them to depart into heaven.

Context provides meaning

Neither "advocate", with its overtones of a court of law, nor "comforter", which fails to suggest any form of instruction or guidance, adequately translates the ideas that are introduced by the word *parakletos*. The breadth of meaning that is involved starts to be revealed when the word is understood in the context of the passages where it appears. In 1 John 2:1, for example, it is "if any man sin" that the abiding presence of an "advocate" is so important. This is not to suggest that, like an offender retaining the best possible lawyer to plead his cause, the Lord will cleverly argue to reduce the severity of the sentence for believers who sin, but that repentant sinners can be reassured of the efficacy of Christ's saving work. The presence of the Lord Jesus in heaven is the unmistakable guarantee that God is "faithful and just to forgive us our sins and to cleanse us from all unrighteousness" (1 John 1:9).

When it is used in John's Gospel, the word includes other shades of meaning. The idea of "comfort" is certainly there, in the promise that the disciples would not be bereft (e.g., John 14:16). But there are also the ideas of teaching, witnessing and testifying to the truth of the Lord's word (see 14:26; 15:26).

The use of a related word in an incident at the time of Jesus' birth strengthens this message. God's people were in darkness; His word had been silent for four hundred years. Yet there were faithful individuals here and there, like aged Simeon, "waiting for the consolation (Greek, *paraklesis*) of Israel" (Luke 2:25). God's response was the gift of His Son, "a light to bring revelation to the Gentiles, and the glory of your people Israel" (verse 32). Simeon must have prayed earnestly for the fulfilment of God's purpose, and God comforted him with the wonderful message of salvation through Christ.

The comfort of the Holy Spirit

Those living after Christ's earthly ministry were also consoled. The evidence of his victory over sin and death was provided by his resurrection, and the knowledge that the Lord sits at the Father's right hand confirms that believers too are brought into "heavenly places in Christ Jesus" (Ephesians 2:6). A brief comment in Acts shows how the living Lord transforms the lives of his disciples:

"Then the churches throughout all Judea, Galilee, and Samaria had peace and were edified. And walking in the fear of the Lord and in the comfort (Greek, *paraklesis*) of the Holy Spirit, they were multiplied." (Acts 9:31)

For the apostles, the certainty of the Lord's abiding comfort was guaranteed when they received the power of the Holy Spirit. This provided them an accurate recollection of all that Jesus did and taught whilst he was with them, and confirmed by miraculous works the message they preached in his name.

Subsequent generations benefit from this work. There now exists an authentic account of the Lord's ministry, describing what he did, what he taught, and his demeanour as he moved through Judea and Galilee preaching the Gospel of the kingdom. The Apostle John commented at the end of his Gospel account that, despite many more incidents that could have been recorded, "these are written that you may believe that Jesus is the Christ, the Son of God, and that believing you may have life through his name" (John 20:31). All who live distant in time or geography from first century Palestine are therefore not deficient in any way in terms of the information that is available about the Lord's work. His guidance speaks as clearly from the pages of scripture today as did his words spoken from a fishing boat moored by the edge of a lake two thousand years ago.

"Lo, I am with you always"

Prayerful meditation on Jesus' teaching calls him alongside at any time, in any situation and any location. This is another vitally important aspect of holding fast to our Head, who is Christ. How foolish we should be to ignore the help and comfort he offers! The enormous benefit felt by his first century disciples from his physical presence with them indicates what is available spiritually to believers today through the privilege of prayer and meditation on the Word of life.

It is surely significant that in his letter to the ecclesia in Laodicea written to the "lukewarm" disciples who met together there, Jesus wrote: "Behold, I stand at the door and knock. If anyone hears my voice and opens the door, I will come in to him ..." (Revelation 3:20). Brothers and sisters in Laodicea prided themselves on their worldly prosperity, and were ignorant of the reality of their situation, which the Lord could see. In his sight they were "wretched, miserable, poor, blind, naked". In their blindness they were not aware that Jesus was ever present to be called alongside as Comforter and Guide. He revealed moreover that his availability was not simply passive, as if he was ready to respond only if they called first. "I stand at the door *and knock*", he said. This required them to listen, and so turn to him for help. But it explains that the initiative is his. It is no different today. The Lord is at the door, and is knocking. We must listen to his words and example revealed in the scriptures, for these loudly proclaim his desire to assist.

Yet this assistance is not available if we ignore the truth he taught, or fail to reflect his teachings or heed his guidance. Those qualifications previously mentioned are crucial. Prayer is offered "in his name"; approach is made to God "through him". When this happens, his words to his disciples are true for all believers, "Lo, I am with you always, even to the end of the age" (Matthew 28:20).

12

NOT TURNING BACK

THROUGHOUT the pages of scripture runs a theme of keeping one's sight fixed firmly on the goal ahead, and not turning aside from it. As he gave the children of Israel commandments to order their lives as the people of God, Moses said: "You shall be careful to do as the LORD your God has commanded you; you shall not turn aside to the right hand or to the left" (Deuteronomy 5:32). God does not deviate from His purpose, and He expected that His people would also be singleminded in their attempts to follow His ways.

In particular they were to acknowledge His supremacy. "You shall have no other gods before me" was God's first commandment to the Israelites (Exodus 20:3), and He warned them against turning aside after idols: "you shall not turn aside from any of the words which I command you this day, to the right or to the left, to go after other gods to serve them" (Deuteronomy 28:14).

Because of the clear direction that derives from God's word, the wise father instructed his son: "Let your eyes look straight ahead, and your eyelids look right before you. Ponder the path of your feet, and let all your ways be established. Do not turn to the right or the left: remove your foot from evil" (Proverbs 4:25-27).

The example of God Himself is thus upheld for men and women to follow.

"Every good gift and every perfect gift is from above, and comes down from the Father of lights, with whom there is no variation or shadow of turning."   (James 1:17)

No turning back

Because God is upright and direct in His ways, the same characteristics are required of His creatures. As Jesus said: "No one, having put his hand to the plough, and looking back, is fit for the kingdom of God" (Luke 9:62). Turning aside, turning back, or turning away from the set path is equivalent to denying what God has done and is doing for mankind. Consistency is the great hallmark of all that God does; He never turns back. Reflecting on this the Psalmist spoke of what he was able to do once God's gentleness had made him great:

"I have pursued my enemies and overtaken them; neither did I turn back again till they were destroyed." (Psalm 18:37)

God was Father, King and Husband to Israel. He was their Shepherd; where He led, they were to follow. But so often, Israel failed. God was not kept at the forefront of their minds, and they found the deceitful worship of idols more immediately satisfying. By not upholding God's majesty, they did not uphold His ways; and they began to serve images "made like corruptible man – and birds and four-footed animals and creeping things" (Romans 1:23). A deep, moral sickness affected mankind, and man was adrift on a stormy ocean where he could no longer see any landmarks to guide him to safety.

In accordance with God's warning to His people, foreign powers entered the land of Israel, taking captive first the northern and then the southern kingdom. Some were asking, as they have on occasions since, "Has God cast away his people?" (Romans 11:1). So God revealed through one of His prophets a vision of His unchangeable purpose, which cannot be frustrated by man's failure. Ezekiel, sitting "among the captives by the River Chebar ... saw visions of God" (Ezekiel 1:1). The vision was literally fantastic: the chariot of Israel, such as Elisha saw when Elijah was taken from him (cp. 2 Kings 2:11,12). As we might expect of a divine vehicle, "each one went *straight forward*; they went

67

wherever the spirit wanted to go, and *they did not turn when they went*" (Ezekiel 1:12).

A remnant shall be saved

Ezekiel was being shown that, despite the nation being taken into captivity, God's purpose with mankind would continue with individuals. The purpose still involved the hope of Israel, for the vision was of "the chariot of Israel" (as the four cherubic faces revealed), but depended on the response of individuals, irrespective of race, gender or status. Was not the prophet in the heart of an idolatrous land: territory marked from the earliest times as a centre for those who oppose God? Yet God was working even there for the salvation of a faithful remnant, and those with the eye of faith could see Him.

This is not the place for a detailed exposition of Ezekiel 1 and 10, the chapters that record what the prophet saw. But there are important features of his vision that help to illuminate the theme of holding fast to our head, who is Christ. First of all, the divine chariot was fully equipped to be victorious. Its large wheels were well able to override any enemy, and additionally there were wings so that its movements were not restricted to the earth. The Lord similarly was equipped to vanquish man's greatest enemy: he had access to the word of God, and as God's Son he thrilled to its message, applying it to every situation he faced. He lived constantly in the knowledge that God's power was available for his use. As he said to Peter: "do you think that I cannot now pray to my Father, and he will provide me with more than twelve legions of angels?" (Matthew 26:53). Like the chariot of Israel, Jesus never diverted from the path assigned to him, "he stedfastly set his face to go to Jerusalem" (Luke 9:51).

A perfect man

The chariot that Ezekiel saw was not, however, a single individual but a great company of powerful beings, that had "the likeness of a man" (Ezekiel 1:5). In this sense, his vision forms a basis for the Apostle's description of

68

the "perfect man" into whom believers grow when they acknowledge Christ as their head (Ephesians 4:12-16). This becomes apparent in the further description of the cherubim in Ezekiel chapter 10. Again describing the divine characteristic of the chariot of Israel not being diverted from its purpose, the prophet uses a different expression from the one that occurs in chapter 1. There he spoke of the great company going wherever the spirit would lead them: "each one went straight forward; they went wherever the spirit wanted to go, and they did not turn when they went" (Ezekiel 1:12). In chapter 10 a different expression is used: "they did not turn aside when they went, but followed in the direction the head was facing" (verse 11). They followed the head, whom the Apostle confirms is Christ.

In this context, therefore, the Spirit expresses the divine purpose and intention revealed in vision to the prophet. This purpose was declared as Israel's hope: a hope that would be fulfilled through the work of the Saviour-King, bringing victory over man's enemy – sin – and leading captivity captive. The Apostle was also inspired to see this great truth when he meditated on the prophetic writings. He read, for example, the words of Isaiah, "Who has directed the Spirit of the LORD, or as his counselor has taught him?" (Isaiah 40:13), and saw how they were fulfilled in Christ: "For 'who has known the mind of the Lord that he may instruct him?' But we have the mind of Christ" (1 Corinthians 2:16).

To become part of God's developing purpose, and to share in the glories of the future age, believers must stay close to their head, following wherever he leads. We only stay close to him by systematically developing his mind. His mind was centred on his Father's word, and was moulded by it, which is the only way we can direct our minds to heavenly and not to earthly things. We live in an age full of distractions and diversions, and confess how difficult it is to remain singleminded and devoted.

69

Wholehearted commitment
This is where the examples of Israel and of Christ can assist. All those passages about not turning aside now have an application for us as well as for God's nation. First and foremost is the need to acknowledge God's supremacy, as Jesus always did. There can be no doubt that this applies also to us, for the Lord Jesus confirmed it: "'You shall love the Lord your God with all your heart, with all your soul, with all your mind, and with all your strength.' This is the first commandment" (Mark 12:30).

The consequence of allowing the Father to rule in our lives is to allow Him to direct our thoughts and actions through Christ. The Apostle described how this is a constant task: "We even fight to capture every thought until it acknowledges the authority of Christ" (2 Corinthians 10:5, J. B. Phillips). As we need to love God with *all* our heart, mind, soul and strength, so we must attempt to capture *every* thought in recognition of the Lord's headship. We must seek always to follow where the head leads.

Israel felt burdened under God's requirements, and that burden has been removed for us by Christ. The burden has been removed, but His commandments remain. They should be seen by the followers of the Lord Jesus as a joyous service, and as helping us to stay close to him: "for this is the love of God, that we keep his commandments. And his commandments are not burdensome" (1 John 5:3).

The vision speaks
What Ezekiel learned in his captivity was the certainty of God's purpose. His will cannot be thwarted by man, and at the appointed time the earth will be filled with His glory. Those who follow where His purpose leads will be included among His saints, through whom that glory will be revealed. Association with the divinely appointed head is the key. Whatever personal need may arise can be answered by developing his mind: "he will be very gracious to you at the sound of your cry; when

he hears it, he will answer you ... your ears shall hear
a word behind you, saying, 'This is the way, walk in it,'
whenever you turn to the right hand or whenever you
turn to the left" (Isaiah 30:19-21).

13

LOOSING HOLD

THE comments of onlookers and observers about disciples of the Lord Jesus Christ make fascinating reading. There was the occasion when members of the Jewish council were faced with the problem of what to do with the apostles who refused to be silent about what they had seen and heard, and who taught fearlessly and openly in Jerusalem. "When they saw the boldness of Peter and John, and perceived that they were uneducated and untrained men, they marvelled. And they realised that they had been with Jesus" (Acts 4:13).

The two apostles were marked out because of a strong similarity to the Lord they sought to serve. This cannot have been a physical likeness even though they were all from Galilee, but was related to their demeanour. Like him, they would not bow to any pressure to remain silent. As Peter said on the occasion of a subsequent arrest by the Jewish authorities, "We ought to obey God rather than men" (5:29).

Later, a more cosmopolitan group of disciples met together regularly in Syrian Antioch, forming a vibrant and energetic team. They too displayed a visible relationship to the Lord, such that "the disciples were first called Christians in Antioch" (11:26). Those who witnessed their activities perceived them to be Christ's men and Christ's women. The description may have been intended originally as a term of rebuke, but it revealed a wonderful truth about the Lord's disciples.

Cutting worldly ties
Peter and John were Galilean fishermen, but they left their past behind to become fishers of men. They were

not formally educated, but they spoke with confidence and conviction about the things they believed. The new converts in Antioch were from many different nationalities and different walks of life, yet they became associated with the Lord Jesus so closely that people in Antioch did not call them Syrians, Cyrenians, Cypriots or Jews but Christians. Both incidents teach a critical and important message. If disciples are to hold fast to their head, they must loose their hold on previous ties and associations.

How to live as a disciple of Christ in a godless world is a subject that has exercised men and women down the centuries. Some religious groups believe that it is necessary to cut off virtually all contact with the rest of humanity, living behind monastery walls, and in extreme cases refraining from all verbal contact – even with those who are similarly separated. This ignores the thrust of the Lord's teaching, contained in his great intercessory prayer before his final sacrifice:

"I have given them your word; and the world has hated them because they are not of the world, just as I am not of the world. I do not pray that you should take them out of the world, but that you should keep them from the evil one. They are not of the world, just as I am not of the world. Sanctify them by your truth. Your word is truth."   (John 17:14-17)

Not of the world

The experiences of Peter and John with the Jewish authorities perfectly mirror the Lord's words. The Jewish leaders hated them because they were not of the world of Jewry, and presented a message that struck at its foundations. God did not remove them from all possibility of opposition, but their conviction that His word is true set them apart, and kept them from the evil schemes of godless men:

"For the wrath of God is revealed from heaven against all ungodliness and unrighteousness of men, who suppress (hold down, RV) the truth in un-righteousness."   (Romans 1:18)

This situation did not happen overnight; the disciples did not show unshakeable confidence from the moment they first started to accompany Jesus as he preached. The accounts in the Gospels reveal how they lurched between times of confidence and periods of despair. They were strong when the Lord was present, and incredibly vulnerable when he was absent. Away from his presence they were not holding fast to their head, and they slipped back to the position where they were no different from their contemporaries in the world.

The eye of faith

Immediately after his outstanding declaration of Jesus' Sonship, Peter's faith weakened when he heard the Lord speaking of the treatment the Jewish leaders would mete out to him when he visited Jerusalem; he could not accept that false accusations, torture and execution formed part of God's purpose for His Son, and for a time he did not believe the Lord's words: his hold loosened. Under difficult circumstances when he took the enormous personal risk of going into the high priest's palace under cover of darkness, he was suddenly exposed by an unexpected challenge:

"Then he began to curse and swear, saying, 'I do not know the man!' Immediately a rooster crowed. And Peter remembered the word of Jesus who had said to him, 'Before the rooster crows, you will deny me three times.' So he went out and wept bitterly."

(Matthew 26:74,75)

What a change from this broken and dejected fisherman to the bold and confident preacher six weeks later on the day of Pentecost! Peter had learned how to hold fast to the head, who is Christ and thus to loosen his hold on the world and its ways. "Faith is the substance of things hoped for, the evidence of things not seen" (Hebrews 11:1), and therefore Peter was able to see that the Jewish leaders' confidence was misplaced; their position of authority and power was surely crumbling and would soon disappear completely. He served a greater leader, to whom all other powers must be subject. Peter and the apostles now had a completely different perspective on life. Outwardly they lived as they had done previously: their homes were no different, they ate the same food and wore the same clothes as their contemporaries, and they kept the same occupations they had when Jesus called them. The direction of their lives could not, however, be more different. They were no longer anxious about the trappings of daily life, and were more concerned with life itself. Their hope centred on the promise of eternal life, which caused them to view every aspect of daily life through the Lord's eyes.

Their experiences are recorded for our benefit and instruction, for we are also being called to hold fast to the head who is Christ, and to loosen our hold on the things of the world. As the examples we have considered show, we are not asked to cut our ties with the world in order to be free to hold fast to Christ – that would put the cart before the horse. It would be like the man in Jesus' parable who was cleansed of an evil spirit and rejoicing in his liberty put nothing in its place; he was later inhabited by seven other spirits more wicked than himself (Luke 11:24-26). The lesson appears to be that the closer we can draw to the Lord, the more our former worldly ties are loosed; the more we can fill ourselves with him and become like him, the more we shall be his representatives. Loosing can only be achieved by tightening the hold on something greater.

Birth of the new man

The Apostle Paul suggests that the process is something like childbirth, as if the new man in Christ is a foetus growing in the womb of the old man of the earth from which eventually it will be free. He wrote to the Galatians about his earnest prayer on their behalf: "My little children, for whom I labour in birth again until Christ is formed in you" (Galatians 4:19). Like many processes the progress will not always be steady and consistent. Each disciple will confess that faith waxes and wanes; the world's hold seems more insistent on some days than others; temptations can be overcome easily on one occasion, but lead quickly to sin in times of weakness.

, The antidote to temptation is always available; it exists in the word and example of the Lord Jesus. Each disciple living in the world is bombarded by worldly thinking, and with no defences to resist its insistent messages that thinking produces worldly children. The faithful disciple knows that "the form (fashion, KJV) of this world is passing away" (1 Corinthians 7:31) and thus he strives to become an onlooker rather than a participant.

Worldly attractions

Like righteous Lot, true disciples are tormented on a daily basis by the things they see and hear in the world around them. It was always so –

"for the flesh lusts against the Spirit, and the Spirit against the flesh; and these are contrary to one another." (Galatians 5:17)

The time to worry is when the world looks attractive, and we fail to see its wickedness or hear its blasphemies; when we say there is no harm in things that have no goodness. This is a sure sign that the hold on the Lord has slipped and the world's hold has tightened again.

The insistent beat of worldliness must, however, be countered by the powerful message of truth. Jesus said that we "cannot serve God and mammon" (Matthew 6:24): we cannot hold on to him and to the world, for that would tear us in two. There is a broad path and a narrow path – one to destruction, and the other to safety (7:13,14). The life of discipleship demands that we strive to walk ever more closely with the Lord. Victories over temptations are then his, and not ours. He extends the consolation of forgiveness when we stray and return to him. He constantly searches out his wandering sheep.

By seeking always to hold tightly to the Lord, he gradually prises us away from our former dependence on worldly ambition and rewards, offering what none of us deserves, even everlasting life in his Father's kingdom.

14

IS CHRIST DIVIDED?

EARLIER chapters have commented on the shared and complementary aims of the Head and the body, by applying the apostolic analogy of the human body and its different parts to the Lord Jesus Christ and his saints. Holding closely to the Head also involves therefore holding fast to the members of Christ's body, his worldwide ecclesia.

But occasions arise in ecclesial life where individuals find themselves out of step with their brothers and sisters, sometimes to the point where they decide the issue is so serious they can no longer walk together. The question arises in this situation – Who is still holding to the Head: those who separate from the ecclesia, or the remainder who are left behind? Undoubtedly, both parties will claim that they seek to uphold the Lord's example, and are faithful to his commands, but is it really possible for both to be holding to him?

The seriousness of separation from the ecclesia lies in the fact that in practical terms it means individuals are separated from the rest of the body. What no one other than the Lord can determine is whether the relationship with him is also affected. But it is certainly far from ideal.

Troubles in Corinth

The apostle Paul commented on a situation like this in his first letter to the ecclesia in Corinth, after learning about the deep divisions that were causing confusion in ecclesial meetings. He posed the question, "Is Christ divided?" (1 Corinthians 1:13). In the ultimate sense, of course, there is only one answer to this. Christ is not, and cannot be divided. When he returns to gather the

78

saints to him, he will be united forever with the faithful, and will separate himself eternally from the unfaithful. To a large degree, the apostle was asking a rhetorical question. But this great truth must not be used to ignore the danger of human factions, as if the existence of different groups within an ecclesia is unimportant because Christ cannot be divided. The apostle's concern about affairs in first century Corinth indicates that whereas Christ cannot be divided, his body often is, and it is deeply shameful whenever and wherever it occurs.

Paul counselled the Corinthians to settle their differences and work together for the benefit of the whole ecclesia. By realising that it is wrong to tear Christ's body apart, each individual brother and sister was thus encouraged to "Make love your aim" (14:1, RSV). The argument he used is compellingly simple: ecclesias are made up of weak, insignificant and mortal individuals who have been called to God's eternal purpose. In their association with Him through the Lord Jesus Christ, His majesty and power must always be remembered, so that "no flesh should glory in his presence" (1:29). Rather than the self-centred attitude that often underlies divisive behaviour, Paul advised another group of believers in Rome to "pursue the things which make for peace and the things by which one may edify another" (Romans 14:19).

Separation

This does not mean that it is always wrong to separate. Fellowship, both with the Father and the Son, and with fellow believers, is based on sharing the saving elements of the one faith (1 John 1:1-4). Where these elements are no longer believed and upheld, the grounds of fellowship no longer exist. Such a situation occurred some time after the completion of the New Testament. The early ecclesias had members who fell away from the truth, as predicted by the apostles, who eventually formed an apostate church: "They went out from us, but they were not of us; for if they had been of us, they would have continued with us; but they went out that they might be made manifest, that none of them were of us" (1 John 2:19). No true believer would countenance fellowshipping with any who deny that Christ came in the flesh and will return to establish God's kingdom upon the earth, or who say that temptation comes from a supernatural evil being.

No, the separation that was threatening to occur in Corinth was between brothers and sisters who shared the same fundamentals of faith, but were being driven apart by secondary issues. These secondary matters each had their advocates, so that separate parties or factions were grouping around and becoming identified with specific individuals. Disagreements between the factions were driving them even further apart.

Paul appealed to them, "by the name of our Lord Jesus Christ, that you all speak the same thing, and that there be no divisions among you, but that you be perfectly joined together in the same mind and in the same judgment" (1 Corinthians 1:10). Whatever differences existed, they were not sufficient in the apostle's assessment to justify either serious disagreement or separation. What then were these secondary matters? The list of problems that were besetting the ecclesia in Corinth was long and serious, ranging from misunderstandings over the teaching of the resurrection, to refusing to take action over a case of gross immorality. The apostle's counsel was clear; many of these issues arose because of endemic disunity in the ecclesia, rather than being the underlying cause of the disunity. If the brothers and sisters would give more consideration to the needs of all members of the ecclesia, drawing more closely to the example of the Lord Jesus by giving all honour to God, even the most difficult issues could be properly discussed and faithfully resolved. The ecclesia had reached a position of stalemate where every new issue revealed the presence of serious fault lines that threatened to tear it apart.

Discord among brethren

Without Paul's letter, it is unlikely that we should consider as "secondary" the serious matters that disturbed the Corinthian ecclesia. Individuals have separated from ecclesias for much less serious reasons; and whole sections have formed separate 'fellowships' over issues that are not intrinsically fundamental. The details of the situation in first century Corinth have therefore been recorded, as were those in Israel of old, "for our admonition, upon whom the ends of the ages have come" (1 Corinthians 10:11). Unless the question that disturbs an ecclesia is truly a foundation principle of the faith, there are no reasonable grounds to justify separation.

God hates discord, and He loves peace. His Son is therefore rightly heir to the title, Prince of Peace, who taught his disciples, "Blessed are the peacemakers: for they shall be called sons of God" (Matthew 5:9, RV). To sow discord, to create schism, to support factious schemes or to separate over matters that are not fundamental runs completely counter to the apostle's advice to the brothers and sisters in Corinth. He wanted them to be peacemakers, following the example of His Son.

Learning about the problems that existed in Corinth, it would have been possible for brothers and sisters in Thessalonica, Berea, Philippi, Athens and wider afield to refuse to have anything to do with the Corinthian ecclesia. Individuals and groups that stand aside from the Christadelphian Central fellowship regularly use this argument. They point to specific problems and difficulties, as if these are reasonable grounds for continuing separation, believing that they justify decisions that were taken long before many of the problems arose. Yet there are no examples in the New Testament of individuals or groups of brothers and sisters being commended for refusing to associate with other ecclesias, even when those ecclesias had serious problems.

No standing aside
Paul was in Ephesus when he wrote to Corinth, but he did not suggest that all Ephesian links with Corinth should be severed until that ecclesia was purged of its difficulties, or that the Ephesians should stand aside for the time being. Instead, the whole tenor of his comments, both to those in Corinth and elsewhere was for brothers and sisters to seek for peace, for unity of thought, and to engage in activities that will strengthen one another through honouring God's name.

In the case of Ephesus – like many other ecclesias in the first century world, comprising believers from Jewish and Gentile stock – ethnic and cultural differences created enormous tensions. The apostle therefore reminded the Ephesian brothers and sisters of the unifying work of Christ. Jews, and Gentiles who were once aliens and strangers from the commonwealth of Israel, were united through "the blood of Christ" (Ephesians 2:11-19). It was a very powerful message, designed to deal with all the wide-ranging differences that can exist between individual believers. If the antipathy between Jews and Gentiles could be reconciled "to God in one body by the cross", what of other causes of difference between brethren and sisters?

The master builder
In his appeals, the Apostle consistently draws attention to the work of Christ. He pleaded with the Corinthians "by the name of our Lord Jesus Christ". He reminded the Ephesians that they were "in Christ Jesus", that he was their peace, and that "one new man" was made "in himself (i.e., in Christ)" where previously there were "two".

Where there are frail human beings, differences will always exist. Differences can easily create divisions, and divisions can lead to separation. Like a fragile piece of bone china, breakages can easily occur, but a shattered pot is virtually impossible to mend: "A brother offended is harder to win than a strong city, and contentions are like the bars of a castle" (Proverbs 18:19). Perhaps humanly speaking a divided and shattered body cannot be repaired. But we cannot ignore the skill of the master-builder. Healing lies in His hands, through the work of His Son, and He appeals to all His children that they may be one, as He is one with the Son.

15

"TO YOUR TENTS, O ISRAEL!"

THE divine comment on the period of the Judges is now proverbial: "In those days there was no king in Israel; everyone did what was right in his own eyes" (Judges 21:25). The words are not complimentary. Selfishness prevailed, and the words "I" and "mine" were far more common than "us" and "ours". An outcome of this selfish attitude can be seen in the preceding verse, where it is recorded, "the children of Israel departed from there at that time, every man to his tribe and family; they went out from there, every man to his inheritance" (verse 24).

Directly contrasting with God's desire for His people to be united in His service, the tribes went man by man to their individual homes. As already indicated, this was not good; it was not good for them, and it was certainly not good nationally. Israel's God is One Lord, and He expects unity to exist among His people.

The irony of the final two verses in Judges is that they follow one of the very few occasions during that sad and sorry epoch in Israel's history when there does seem to have been some concern for the nation as a whole. The decimation of Benjamin after the incident involving the Levite's concubine, aroused deep concern lest "today there should be one tribe missing in Israel" (verse 3). Yet this was only a blip on an otherwise downward path to further and further fragmentation.

Divine test

The preservation of Benjamin, however, meant that when Israel recognised the need for national unity, asking for "a king to judge us like all the nations" (1 Samuel 8:5), God gave them Saul the son of Kish, who was a Benjamite! Such are the ways of Israel's God. Saul's first test came when the cruel Ammonite king Nahash threatened permanently to disfigure the men of Jabesh-gilead, even though they were prepared to serve him. Nahash was determined that his callous barbarity would be a standing reproach against Israel (1 Samuel 11:1,2).

Hearing of this, Saul slaughtered two oxen and sent the bloodied parts throughout Israel to encourage all the tribes to gather and revenge the threat against Jabesh-gilead: "Whoever does not go out with Saul and Samuel to battle, so shall it be done to his oxen" (verse 7). The wonderful response, for the people came out "as one man" (RV), set the scene for how the nation ought to work for the benefit of *all* its inhabitants, and not just for the strong, powerful, or influential.

Saul's successor as king, the beloved king David, understood much better than Saul the importance of a united nation. After Saul's death, where at first only the men of Judah recognised David as their king, the eventual gathering of *"all* the tribes of Israel" to Hebron to make him king has a sense of fitness about it: this is what God wanted (2 Samuel 5:1). Throughout his reign, therefore, David tried to ensure that all the tribes were knit together in a common purpose – against their enemies as well as in worship and praise of their God.

Rebellion

Only when the authority of God's anointed king was challenged do we find the comments from the end of Judges reappearing in the record. Ironically the challenger was a Benjamite, Sheba the son of Bichri, who probably hoped to benefit from his tribal connection with the former king Saul. His revolutionary call was clear and direct, aimed specifically at David but in the process rejecting Israel's God whom he significantly failed to mention: "We have no share in David, nor do we have inheritance in the son of Jesse; every man to his tents, O Israel!" (2 Samuel 20:1).

The unity for which David had struggled long and hard seemed to be unravelling. Evil had arisen out of his own house when Absalom led a rebellion, just as God prophesied after David's sin with Bathsheba, and now there was another rebel. Perhaps David realised how, by his sin, he had given the enemies of the Lord great occasion to blaspheme.

But in raising rebellion against David, and thereby against God too, Sheba had lost his head and his senses. In the events that followed, he also literally lost his head so that the men of Israel who had rallied to his call returned in shame to their own homes, not now as rebels against David but to reflect on the benefits of being ruled by a man after God's own heart from God's throne in Jerusalem.

About fifty years later there was another crisis that threatened Israel's king. David was succeeded first by his son Solomon, and then by Solomon's son Rehoboam. As the people had gathered to David, they gathered again when Rehoboam became king. But they came with a request. They were burdened by the demands laid on them during Solomon's reign, and asked for the burden to be lifted. When Rehoboam followed his younger advisors and promised to increase rather than diminish their burdens, the people took up the words of Sheba the Benjamite, "What share have we in David? We have no inheritance in the son of Jesse. To your tents, O Israel! Now, see to your own house, O David!' So Israel departed to their tents" (1 Kings 12:16).

Challenging God's authority

Despite the implicit warnings of the times of the Judges, Israel preferred their own tents to God's house, which Jeroboam replaced in the northern kingdom by two golden calves, one in Northern Dan, and the other in Bethel. It is difficult to see the action as anything but a direct challenge to God's authority: to erect an idol in a place named the House of God.

These incidents, drawn together in the record by the expression "to your tents, O Israel!", teach very powerful and important lessons for believers in every age who are called to unite together under the headship of the Lord Jesus Christ. Yet time and time again, there are examples of individuals or groups of individuals choosing to remove themselves from the main body – i.e., of the ecclesia, or sometimes even of the whole brotherhood – with a call to all others to go to their tents too.

Family problems

The common feature of all the scriptural examples that have been mentioned is failure to show concern for the good of the whole body, and to promote instead individual desires and wishes – personal comfort and pleasure, perhaps personal profit or even personal power. If this behaviour occurred in families, we would describe the perpetrator as childish or petulant. Consider for a moment a situation in family life. Arrangements have been made for a day's outing. Everyone knows when they are to be ready, but when the time comes one member is disgruntled, and drags his or her heels. Because of some supposed slight, or perhaps from a desire for greater attention, the announcement is made that he is not going: he will stay at home, because he never intended going in the first place! All the arrangements are thrown into confusion; possibly one of the parents stays behind to get to the root of the problem, while the rest of the family go. But the day is spoilt. Those who go on the outing feel they ought not to enjoy themselves, and in reality they can't, because the day is not as enjoyable as it would be if the family were complete. But the one who stays back does not enjoy his day either. If the truth were told, he always wanted to go! His tantrum was signalling some other problem.

Childish behaviour

We expect children to grow out of behaviour like this, so when something similar occurs in ecclesial life we may not immediately draw the comparison. Yet, in all honesty, the brother or sister who stays away from the meetings because of some supposed offence is no different than the petulant child. Like Israel of old, they have returned to their tents.

Unexpected though the behaviour may be, it happens time and again in the experience of ecclesias. As the child knows, the rest of the family want him to be with them. Equally, the brother or sister who stays away knows the rest of the ecclesia will be genuinely unhappy and do all that can be done to restore the equilibrium. Such attention seeking is a way of trying to apply more weight to a position that has failed to gain sufficient support by reasoned discussion. Ecclesias can easily feel pressured when situations like this arise, not knowing the best way to tackle them.

Increasing fragmentation

Something similar occurs when a group of brethren and sisters decide to set up their own ecclesia after an ecclesial issue has not been settled as they would wish. They feel affronted, believing their position is the one with the soundest scriptural support. Yet they failed to convince the majority of the ecclesia. They too return to their tents, and the outcome is an increasingly fragmented family.

When there is a choice of ecclesias within reasonably convenient travelling distance, dissatisfied members in an ecclesia can choose to attend elsewhere, convincing themselves that they are better off among like-minded brothers and sisters. Yet the fact is that, if the issue that caused them to move occurred in the ecclesia they are now attending, it is very possible there would be similar disruption. They believe they have found a safe haven, but the security is almost certainly illusory.

Very rarely do we hear of two or more ecclesias uniting to pool their dwindling resources, or perhaps to maximise the opportunities for preaching. The best reasons for establishing new ecclesias are when existing premises can no longer contain growing numbers, or where a new preaching initiative is beginning to bear fruit. On far too many occasions new ecclesias are simply splinters from an existing ecclesia that have split off because of failure to agree on how to deal with a difficult issue. All this does is signal a serious inability – by all concerned – to give due honour to each other, and particularly to the head. None of these actions solves the root cause of the problem, which is a failure to hold together and a failure to hold the head, which is Christ.

There is a clear lesson, therefore, to be learned from the examples of men who called on Israel to return to their tents. It is a call – wherever it comes from – that is best not heeded. Sometimes we issue the call ourselves, because we have decided to separate from troubles, arguments and difficulty. Sometimes the call comes from another brother or sister, seeking others to join their cause. It is easy under the pressure of difficult circumstances to forget that, at our baptism, we answered a call to join Christ. And we promised to serve him to the end!

16

"CONFESS THE LORD JESUS"

IN his first letter, the Apostle John outlines these two complementary truths about the Lord Jesus Christ:

"We have seen and testify that the Father has sent the Son as Saviour of the world."

"Who ever confesses that Jesus is the Son of God, God abides in him, and he in God." (1 John 4:14,15)

The first of these truths expresses how "God was in Christ reconciling the world to himself" (2 Corinthians 5:19). The primary agent in this reconciliation is God, who, like the father in the parable of the prodigal son, constantly seeks the return of every wayward child. Down through the centuries, God has been calling His children to bring forth fruits meet for repentance. After sending His servants the prophets, "rising early and sending them", and despite the treatment meted out to them, He sent His Son, saying: "probably they will respect him when they see him" (Luke 20:13). People treated Jesus even more harshly than the prophets who preceded him, yet "by the determined purpose and foreknowledge of God", the stripes they inflicted on him healed man's deepest wounds.

Saviour of the world

When John calls Jesus, "the Saviour of the world", there are echoes from two passages in his Gospel. The first of these is well known: "God so loved *the world* that he gave his only begotten Son, that whoever believes in him should not perish but have everlasting life" (John 3:16). The greatest expression of God's love was His sending of the Lord Jesus, to be "the propitiation for our sins, and not for ours only but also for *the whole world*" (1 John 2:2).

The other passage is the account of Jesus' conversation with the woman at the well of Samaria. She returned to her city full of news about the man who told her everything she had done, and asking, "Could this be the Christ?" (John 4:29). Though the people of the city were impressed, and many believed in him, even more became his disciples after Jesus spent two days in their midst: "Now we believe", they said to the woman, "not because of what you said, for we ourselves have heard him and we know that this is indeed the Christ, the Saviour *of the world*" (verse 42). The people who said this were Samaritans; it was not sufficient for them to say that Jesus was Christ, the Jew's Messiah. To save them and other Gentiles he must also be the Saviour of the world. There is possibly also a reference here to an Old Testament incident, for when Pharaoh made Joseph second only to him in Egypt, he gave him a new name: Zaphnath-paaneah (Genesis 41:45). One meaning of this name, according to Jerome (the 4th century scholar who translated the scriptures into Latin), is "Saviour of the World".

The salvation achieved by the Lord therefore has a number of components. First, as the name Jesus suggests, he was God's representative to save his people from their sins (Matthew 1:21), and thus reconcile them to God. Secondly, this salvation is not limited to one group, nation, or people: it is offered to all – the whole world. Then there is the kingdom element. As Joseph cared for the Egyptians, bringing them safely through great tribulation to a time of peace, so the Lord is constantly with his people, leading them in safety to his Father's kingdom.

Apostolic witness

John and the other apostles were witnesses of the Father's purpose in sending His Son; they also became his ambassadors, for he commanded them: "Go into all the world and preach the gospel to every creature"

(Mark 16:15). Peter therefore stood up in Jerusalem on the day of Pentecost and spoke of the death and resurrection of Jesus:

> "This Jesus God has raised up, of which we are all witnesses." (Acts 2:32)

The testimony of the apostles, faithfully recorded by the inspired writers, provides sound grounds for faith, so that "blessed are those who have not seen and yet have believed" (John 20:29).

The fact that God sent Jesus into the world as a saviour requires a response, which is the subject of the second great truth mentioned by John in the passage already quoted. When they hear it, men and women either accept or reject the Gospel of salvation. There is no halfway house, and no ambivalence is acceptable. Either Jesus is the Saviour of the world, or he was an impostor or a charlatan. Acceptance of the message about salvation can only be shown by confession, implying that something more than a mental acknowledgement of its truth is required. This is what the Apostle Paul wrote about confession:

> "If you confess with your mouth the Lord Jesus and believe in your heart that God has raised him from the dead, you will be saved. For with the heart one believes unto righteousness, and with the mouth confession is made unto salvation." (Romans 10:9,10)

Belief and behaviour

There should be no surprise that a person's word and actions must be consistent with his or her beliefs. As Abraham Lincoln once said, "I care not much for a man's religion whose dog and cat are not the better for it". Our association with the Lord Jesus must work a change in us; for beliefs, if they are honestly held, will be evident in a person's pattern of life in things large and small. If, for example, a man believes in "the God of truth" as Isaiah describes the Almighty (Isaiah 65:16), this will produce truthfulness in all aspects of his daily life. Conversely, anyone who lives a life full of deceit, denies the God of truth however strongly he may argue to the contrary.

According to the Apostle Paul, only someone who is "in the Holy Spirit" can truly confess that "Jesus is Lord" (1 Corinthians 12:3, RV). A "holy spirit" in this context is the spirit or mind of the Lord Jesus Christ (see Romans 8:9; 1 Corinthians 2:16; Philippians 2:5), confirming that confession and profession must go hand in hand. Believers in the Lord Jesus should therefore practise what they preach, or more significantly, they should practise and preach what the Lord practised and preached. An observer should be able to tell that, "they had been with Jesus" (Acts 4:13).

Learning from the Lord's example therefore becomes a key factor in holding fast to the Head, who is Christ. Believers rightly claim to be brothers and sisters in him. If he were absent, or if he did not rise from the dead, believers could not be members of his family. Their shared beliefs, particularly in his death and resurrection, create an association that is properly termed "fellowship" – where the binding together of separate individuals is accomplished through shared beliefs, aims and objectives.

The power and strength of fellowship lies in the extent to which individual believers adopt the mind of Christ. If the way they interact with their brothers and sisters reflects how the Lord behaved towards those he met, then their behaviour is "brotherly". But as soon as strife, tensions and backbiting arise, the example of the Head has been forgotten. It is as if believers forget they should be professing Christ, and act according to their base nature, biting and devouring one another. When this occurs, the apostle says, "beware lest you be consumed one of another" (Galatians 5:15).

The message is clear: holding to Christ is constructive and the body is edified. Not to hold to him is destructive both of individuals and of the body itself. Yet far too often, it seems, we learn of dissension, harsh words, cutting off all communication, character assassination and other fleshly manifestations occurring between brothers and sisters. The Lord's words sound a warning here: "By their fruits you will know them" (Matthew 7:20).

"I will dwell in them"

In order to press home its message about the importance of learning from the Lord's example, the quotation this chapter started with does not stop at this point. Speaking of the believer who acknowledges that Christ is his head by confessing that he is the Son of God, the Apostle John adds: "God abides in him, and he in God" (1 John 4:15). Learning from Christ's example, and trying to think, say and do as he did, draws believers closer and closer to God Himself. And the Father, who has always been seeking His wandering children, draws closer too. We learn to dwell, abide, rest and live in God's presence, and He for His part promises to live with His people:

> "You are the temple of the living God. As God has said: 'I will dwell in them and walk among them. I will be their God, and they shall be my people.'"
>
> (2 Corinthians 6:16)

Paul here is quoting Leviticus 26:12 where God explained the benefit to His people of the tabernacle in their midst, the symbol of His continuing presence at the centre of the nation. Moses' tabernacle was merely a shadow of "the true tabernacle which the Lord erected, and not man" (Hebrews 8:2), so the apostle's repetition of the Leviticus passage must be understood in the light of God's work in Christ. Any believer who draws close to the Lord is reassured that through him he is brought near to the Father, and this is expressed in the most amazing terms. First, "God dwells in him", and secondly, "he dwells in God". This can only be true so long as the Lord's example is honoured.

A new commandment

Truly to be sons and daughters of the living God requires that the characteristics of the Lord Jesus

94

should be developed. These are most eloquently displayed, as we have seen, in the fellowship that is shared between his brothers and sisters:

"If someone says, 'I love God,' and hates his brother, he is a liar; for he who does not love his brother whom he has seen, how can he love God whom he has not seen? And this commandment we have from him: that he who loves God must love his brother also." (1 John 4:20,21)

17

THE HEAD OF CHRIST IS GOD

T HE previous chapter concluded that by holding to the Lord Jesus Christ who is our head, we draw closer to him to learn from his example of selfless service, and we also draw closer to his Father who responds by drawing near to each individual believer. We must now take these thoughts to a further and even more exalted stage, for as we are instructed to hold fast to our head who is Christ, it is apparent that throughout his life he held fast to his Head, the Father. "The head of Christ is God", Paul declared unambiguously in the first Corinthian letter (1 Corinthians 11:3). We therefore learn from his example, because his life was patterned wholly and completely on his Father's.

The Lord stated the position uncompromisingly when Jewish rulers were plotting to kill him on the grounds that he had broken the Sabbath Day laws: "The Son can do nothing of himself, but what he sees the Father do", he said, "for whatever he does, the Son also does in like manner" (John 5:19). So completely did Jesus learn from his Father and put into practice what he learned, that he was able to answer Philip's request to be shown the Father, by saying: "Have I been with you so long, and yet you have not known me, Philip? He who has seen me has seen the Father; so how can you say, 'Show us the Father'?" (John 14:9).

"God with us"

This helps to explain the prophecy through Isaiah that was made 700 years before the angel spoke to Joseph when he learned of Mary's miraculous pregnancy: "'Behold, the virgin shall be with child, and bear a son, and they shall call his name Immanuel,' which is translated, 'God with us'" (Matthew 1:23, quoting Isaiah 7:14). While it is true that Jesus was the Son of God because the power of the Highest overshadowed his mother Mary so that the holy child would be God's Son, he became "God with us" only through submitting his will completely to his Father's. Divine characteristics developed in the child through his devotion to the Father's daily spiritual instruction.

Isaiah also prophesied about how the Father's word became the Lord's spiritual diet:

"The Lord GOD ... awakens me morning by morning, he awakens my ear to hear as the learned." (Isaiah 50:4)

Communion with the Father became more important to him than daily food; indeed it was his daily food: "My food is to do the will of him who sent me, and to finish his work", he said (John 4:34). The work was not his, but God's, and he was necessary for its completion.

The child grew

Two verses in the Gospel of Luke combine to explain how the Lord grew and developed both naturally and spiritually. After describing the circumstances of his birth, Luke explains that "the child grew and became strong in spirit, filled with wisdom; and the grace of God was upon him" (Luke 2:40). That the Lord "grew" simply attests to his natural growth from childhood until he entered upon puberty, for the record continues by describing the incident in Jerusalem when Jesus was twelve years old. "Became strong in spirit" refers to his spiritual development, such that even at the age of twelve he was "filled with wisdom". Again the incident in Jerusalem illuminates the account, for when Mary and Joseph found Jesus in the temple, he was "sitting in the midst of the teachers, both listening to them and asking them questions. And all who heard him were astonished at his understanding and answers" (verses 46,47).

97

Luke's final comment is that "the grace (Greek, *charis*) of God was upon him". Some take this as an explanation of Jesus' outstanding understanding and wisdom, as if he had received something directly from the Father that gave him wisdom and understanding. We must note, however, that whereas John the Baptist received the Holy Spirit from his mother's womb, Jesus was not anointed with God's power until the time of his baptism, when he was "about thirty years of age". He did not receive the Spirit therefore until almost twenty years after it was recorded that "the grace of God was upon him".

Another verse in Luke 2 is very helpful in this connection. After returning from Jerusalem to be subject to the family in Nazareth, this further comment is recorded: "Jesus increased in wisdom and stature, and in favour (*charis*) with God and men" (verse 52). Many of the elements of the earlier verse are repeated, as the following table shows:

Luke 2:40	Luke 2:52
the child grew	Jesus increased in … stature
and became strong in spirit, filled with wisdom	(Jesus increased) in wisdom
and the grace of God was upon him	and in favour with God and man

It is apparent from this comparison that "the grace of God" in this context describes the Father's reaction to His Son's development, and not the cause of his spiritual maturity. There is a similar use of the term in Genesis, where it is recorded of Noah that he stood aside from the wickedness of the world before the flood, and therefore "found grace in the eyes of the LORD" (Genesis 6:8). God's response to His Son's obedient understanding and growth in wisdom was later

98

declared audibly on the occasion of his baptism, when "a voice came from heaven which said, 'You are my beloved Son; in you I am well pleased'" (Luke 3:22).

"Thus it becometh us"

The baptism of the Lord was a momentous occasion. Matthew records the conversation between Jesus and John the Baptist when the Lord responded to John's reluctance to baptize him, by saying: "Permit it to be so now, for thus it is fitting for us to fulfill all righteousness" (Matthew 3:15). This declaration showed beyond all doubt that the Lord recognised what God required of him, and what opening up a way of salvation for mankind would mean for him. He saw in his baptism the developing antagonism of the Jewish rulers and their plotting to kill him, he saw the desperate state of mankind immersed in sin and death, he saw the cruel death of the cross, and he saw the glorious resurrection to new life both for himself and for all his faithful disciples.

He had learned of the righteousness of God, and determined throughout his life to reflect that same righteousness day by day. The clarity of his understanding meant that he foresaw every step of the way his Father wanted him to walk, even though this placed an immensely great burden on his shoulders. His knowledge of what the Father had in store for him is revealed in the Gospel of John by references to his "hour", by which he meant the crucial stage of his work when he would lay down his life for others.

My hour has not yet come

He first made the point to his mother Mary, when she asked him to intervene during the wedding feast at Cana at the beginning of his ministry. "Woman", he said, "what does your concern have to do with me? My hour has not yet come" (John 2:4). There is a wedding feast in the purpose of God, and the Lord will both provide and drink wine with his disciples on that occasion, but at the beginning of his ministry a long road lay ahead before that blessed occasion. "My hour has not yet come" spoke of Jesus' determination not to be diverted from the task before him, and of his realisation of how the powers God had given him at baptism were to be used. They were to witness to the truth of the message he taught, rather than be simply dramatic demonstrations of God's power.

Indeed, the personal danger to the Lord of working miracles was emphasised later in his ministry when the Jewish leaders plotted to kill him because he healed on the Sabbath. "They sought to take him; but no one laid a hand on him, because his hour had not yet come" (John 7:30; 8:20).

The Father's agenda was his constant guide, as he openly declared: "I can of myself do nothing. As I hear, I judge; and my judgment is righteous, because I do not seek my own will but the will of the Father who sent me" (John 5:30). The road towards the cross was always a road leading nearer to his Father and the glory of His kingdom: he was growing up into Him. He could see the end always approaching inexorably, until eventually there was one incident that showed he was on the final straight. Every step of the way had been prophesied, and the Jewish scriptures were his constant guide. There was a prophecy of Isaiah's that spoke of God's glory resting on His Messiah. The land would be in deep darkness, and God's people so immersed in their own affairs that they would be blinded to the salvation He offered them. Yet there was hope, and Messiah was encouraged to "Lift up your eyes all around, and see: they all gather together, they come to you; your sons shall come from afar" (Isaiah 60:4). He was shown that "Gentiles shall come to your light, and kings to the brightness of your rising" (verse 3).

"We would see Jesus"

How Jesus must have looked for signs that this prophecy was being fulfilled! The day eventually came when Philip and Andrew told him of some Greeks who were visiting Jerusalem to celebrate Passover, and who had asked to see him. It was the sign he wanted, showing that Gentiles would indeed come to the brightness of his rising. "The hour has come", he said, "that the Son of man should be glorified" (John 12:23).

In his great intercessory prayer, therefore, Jesus acknowledged that the hour had come for his glorification, and in the process God Himself would be glorified:

"Father, the hour has come. Glorify your Son, that your Son also may glorify you."   (John 17:1)

The fact that the Lord consistently sought to honour the Father by listening and responding to His word, both ensured his own future glory, and also glorified God by confirming and acknowledging His eternal purpose. Jesus' example is thus critically important for all his disciples. He always looked to his Head, seeking direction, counsel and strength, and his disciples must do the same. Through always holding firmly to his Father – to His word, His purpose, and His commands – Jesus justified the confidence of all the prophetic comments about what would be achieved by his life of outstanding devotion. The divine response was therefore certain. He was "raised up ... by the glory of the Father" (Romans 6:4).

In the Father's mercy the pattern will continue for all who acknowledge the Headship of Christ, and who hold fast to his wonderful example. As the Apostle wrote: God has "raised us up together, and made us sit together in the heavenly places in Christ Jesus" (Ephesians 2:6).

INDEX OF SCRIPTURE REFERENCES

102

HOLDING THE HEAD